BFI FILM CLASSICS

Edward Busc[illegible]

SERIES ED[illegible]

Cinema is a fragile medium. Many of the great classic films of the past now exist, if at all, in damaged or incomplete prints. Concerned about the deterioration in the physical state of our film heritage, the National Film Archive, a Division of the British Film Institute, has compiled a list of 360 key films in the history of the cinema. The long-term goal of the Archive is to build a collection of perfect showprints of these films, which will then be screened regularly at the Museum of the Moving Image in London in a year-round repertory.

BFI Publishing has now commissioned a series of books to stand alongside these titles. Authors, including film critics and scholars, film-makers, novelists, historians and those distinguished in the arts, have been invited to write on a film of their choice, drawn from the Archive's list. Each volume will present the author's own insights into the chosen film, together with a brief production history and a detailed filmography, notes and bibliography. The numerous illustrations have been specially made from the Archive's own prints.

With new titles published each year, the BFI Film Classics series will rapidly grow into an authoritative and highly readable guide to the great films of world cinema.

42nd Street opens in Kansas City

BFI FILM CLASSICS

42ND STREET

J. Hoberman

BFI PUBLISHING

First published in 1993 by the
BRITISH FILM INSTITUTE
21 Stephen Street, London W1P 1PL

British Library Cataloguing in Publication Data

Hoberman, J
42nd Street –
I. Title II. Series
791.43

ISBN 0-85170-355-0

Designed by
Andrew Barron & Collis Clements Associates

Typesetting by
Fakenham Photosetting Limited, Norfolk

Printed in Great Britain by
The Trinity Press, Worcester

CONTENTS

For Anna Hoberman,
Mara Hoberman, Dorothy Hoberman,
and Ruby Keeler

ACKNOWLEDGMENTS

Production stills were provided by Eastman House. Thanks to Chris Horak. Frame stills provided by the BFI Stills, Posters and Designs Department.

Ruby Keeler on set

I

> Should the street be considered as one of the fine arts?
>
> Fernand Léger (1928)

'Naughty, bawdy, gaudy, sporty', *42nd Street* is a prime chunk of fantasy real-estate – not just a movie, but a novel, a song, a play, an act, an attitude, a dream, a racket, a rhythm, a way of life.

42nd Street is the hectic intersection where industrial folklore crosses show business myth. It's the tale of how America licked the Depression, how the Warner Brothers elected Franklin Roosevelt, and how Hollywood got to out-sing, out-dance, and out-entertain Broadway. Indeed, America's pre-eminent theatrical strip, the thoroughfare in 'the heart of little old New York' that gives *42nd Street* its name, was well in decline on 9 March 1933 when the movie's theme first blared out and its iconic title filled the screen at the Strand Theatre, five blocks away.

Times Square, where 42nd Street crosses Broadway, had once been the best-lit stage in American culture. But as burlesque, vaudeville and second-run movies replaced legitimate shows, *Variety* declared that the 'gayest, white wayest and most expensive nite life street in the world' had turned 'cut-rate'. It was as though the street predicted its own democratisation – or should we say, Warnerisation. For even before the studio produced *42nd Street*, Warner Bros was the celebrant of that particular turf, the purveyor of brash, racy, cynical, up-to-date movies populated by fast-talking wise-guys – shysters and news-hounds, racketeers and their molls.

42nd Street 'has the lean, hungry, underlit look of Warners' films of the same era,' writes Rocco Fumento in his introduction to the 1980 publication of the movie's screenplay. The sets are threadbare, the costumes look to be strictly off-the-rack. Even the musical extravaganzas seem frugal: 'The "Young and Healthy" number has a lot of chorus boys and girls but no setting whatsoever except for three revolving platforms.' But that squadron of chorines and those motorised platforms tell all: *42nd Street* is the Times Square of the assembly line.

This is a street movie where there are almost no street scenes – and then they are mainly rear-projected stock shots as seen from a stage-door or a taxi window. The street here is a state of mind. The stage in *42nd Street* is the distillation of the street, the spectacle is the making of the show, and the show itself is a model metropolis – the nexus of glamorous display, fantastic abundance, and utopian social order.

Early in the twentieth century, stimulated by the completion of the Times Building and the opening of the subway, New York's amusement centre moved uptown from 14th Street to the Times Square area. There were already seven theatres on 42nd Street, between Seventh and Eighth Avenues, when in December 1905 the *Dramatic Mirror* proclaimed the block the city's 'New Rialto'. The theatres of 42nd Street now show mainly pornography, but the names of those impresarios who once ruled them retain a certain mouldy grandeur: Oscar Hammerstein, David Belasco, the Shubert brothers, George White, Earl Carroll and, above all, Florenz Ziegfeld, who in July 1907 staged the first edition of his annual *Follies* at the same Liberty Theatre where, eight years later at unprecedented prices, D.W. Griffith would open *The Birth of a Nation*.

Ziegfeld was the most celebrated American showman since P.T. Barnum and he similarly believed in overstimulating his audience. The *Follies* were a veritable entertainment machine. 'The revue shows a mania for perfection,' Gilbert Seldes wrote in an early appreciation of Ziegfeld.

> It aspires to precise and definite, it corresponds to those *de luxe* railway trains which are always exactly on time, to the ease of commerce when there is a fixed price; jazz or symphony may sound from the orchestra pit, but underneath is the real tone of the revue, the steady, incorruptible purr of the dynamo.

But if speed and timing dominated, pretty young women in daring outfits were the main attraction. Ziegfeld not only retooled the chorus line from static ensemble into a precision mechanism, he 'glorified' his chorus girls as glamorously wholesome creatures. The basest form of display (women in tights posed as 'living statuary' in all-male saloons) was now an experience designed for mixed audiences and the highest social strata. Indeed, it was a representation of American technological power and industrial opulence. The rational, engineered 'dynamo' of the clockwork-perfect chorus line amplified the economic drive of the so-called tired businessmen who sat before it.

Most frequently described as 'kaleidoscopic', the *Follies* distilled and choreographed the fleeting impressions of metropolitan life. Non-metropolitan Americans viewed New York with fascinated revulsion, as a vaguely foreign place of mad competition and moral pollution, a trap for the unwary. But in the *Follies*, the metropolis implied a self-actualising liberation. 'The Girl From My Home Town', the opening number of the 1915 edition, showed young women from all over America converging on New York. Ziegfeld chorines were not only the personification of 1920s prosperity, but also the sublimation of the independent working women, shopgirls and stenographers who had joined the urban labour force during the first decades of the twentieth century.

The ideal chorus girl was a Horatio Alger heroine, an American Cinderella, free to sing and dance her way up the staircase of success. Ziegfeld gave this self-serving myth its definitive form in his 1920 extravaganza *Sally*, with Marilyn Miller playing an impoverished orphan who ascends through the chorus to an earthly paradise of fame, wealth and romantic love. 'Dreams nurtured by the big cities,' writes Siegfried Kracauer, 'materialised as pictorial records of chance meetings, strange overlappings, and fabulous coincidences.'

The 1925–6 season was the peak – it was estimated then that each evening some 750,000 people passed through Times Square in search of entertainment – but the invention of the talkies sent an electric charge through the old theatres. Warner Bros, MGM and Paramount all opened sound studios in New York City. The American movie industry was briefly bi-coastal: as late as 1930 *Variety* predicted that, thanks to sound, most production would return to New York.

The magic name was 'Ziegfeld' (or as the 1929 MGM musical *Broadway Melody* calls him, 'Zanfield'). The old Ziegfeld productions, *Rio Rita* and *Sally*, as well as his current hit *Whoopee!*, were rushed into production. Warners advertised their *Broadway Babies* for its 'honest-to-Ziegfeld songs and dances'. Universal, Fox and Paramount were each wooing the great man to give up the stage and produce talking pictures. Independent producer Sam Goldwyn openly coveted his title.

The movies promised Ziegfeld for the masses – even Ziegfeld was

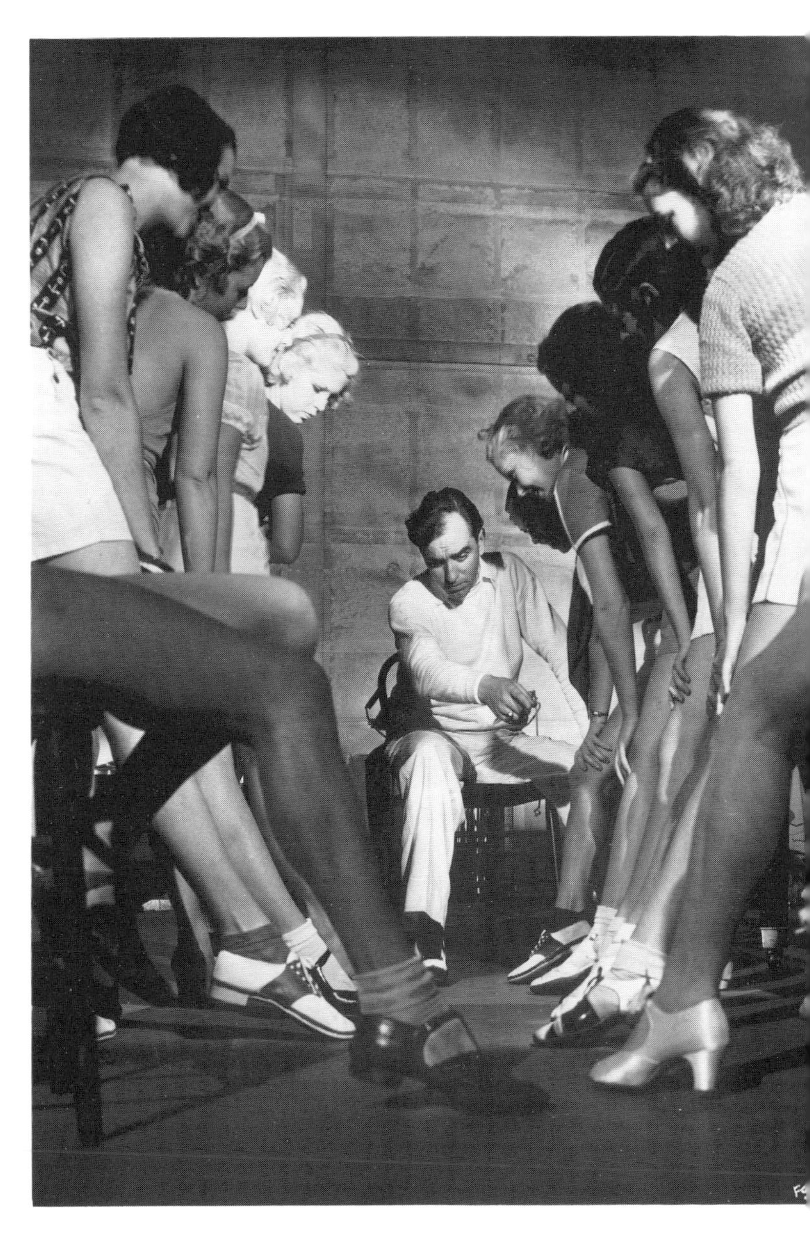

A characteristic publicity shot of Busby Berkeley and chorines

intrigued. As early as the summer of 1926, he had explored the possibility of a Famous Players–Lasky version of the *Follies* to be called *Glorifying the American Girl*. Jesse Lasky rejected the project when it costed out at $1.6 million, but this ill-fated production was revived at Paramount weeks after *The Jazz Singer* opened, going through twenty-five rewrites, repeated shifts in director and cast, and hundreds of thousands of dollars (with Ziegfeld himself drawing $1,000 per week) before its lugubrious account of – what else? – a shopgirl who becomes a Follies star finally materialised (and flopped) three years later. That was two months after Ziegfeld, among others, was wiped out in the stock market crash.

More auspicious was *Whoopee!*, the million-dollar, two-strip Technicolor Ziegfeld–Goldwyn collaboration that, at the suggestion of star Eddie Cantor, had brought dance director Busby Berkeley to Hollywood and thus initiated the mechanisation of the Broadway revue – a chapter in the history of sex and technology as well as show business. Berkeley went to California to become the spirit of 42nd Street, to marry (as Gerald Mast put it) the Ziegfeld showgirl to the crane used by Griffith to traverse the epic Babylon set for *Intolerance*.

Berkeley was in fact originally from Los Angeles, born William Berkeley Enos, the child of a stage director and a diva. His mother's success allowed for his education in an Eastern military academy. He enlisted in the army and was shipped to France where, as a second lieutenant and then as entertainment officer under General Pershing, he choreographed and conducted all manner of military marches, manoeuvres and parade drills. Back home, young Enos turned professional actor, taking his mother's name and enjoying some success on Broadway during the mid-1920s as the comically effeminate London fashion designer Madame Lucy in the long-running revival of the musical *Irene*.

While playing Madame Lucy, Berkeley staged dances for several shows and also assisted Sammy Lee, choreographer for the *Ziegfeld Follies*. His break came in 1927, when he directed the dance numbers for Lew Fields's production of the Rogers and Hart musical *A Connecticut Yankee in King Arthur's Court*. (It's fitting that this adaptation of Mark Twain's novel should have been a Berkeley milestone; the book also furnished the phrase 'new deal' which, thanks to Franklin Roosevelt, would ultimately affix itself to Berkeley's cinematic breakthrough.)

Descriptions of Berkeley's stage work bring to mind accounts of the Tiller Girls, the precision dance troupe that dazzled Weimar Berlin; those 'products of American "distraction factories"', as Kracauer called them, 'no longer individual girls, but indissoluble female units whose movements are mathematically demonstrations.' Somewhat less theoretical, Berkeley's reviews cite the 'zestful, breathless prancing' of the 'excellently drilled [and] comely chorus', noting that their 'gymnastics are remarkable, not so much for the ladies' mechanical perfection as for the great variety of very charming and very original arrangements.'

'Rialto Fame Comes Suddenly to Young Director of Dances,' the *New York Herald-Tribune* reported on 20 November 1927.

> The technique applied by Mr Berkeley is difficult to explain, it being a combination of the classic, jazz, buck, acrobatic and pageant. For instance, one of the first numbers in the show is with a chorus in modern dress, a conglomeration of steps which combines jazz with individuality, a Charleston effect with acrobatic leaps. It is a rushing, twirling affair with a tom-tom beat, leaving the chorus breathless and the audience applauding.

Present Arms, the next season's Rogers and Hart show, was ready-made for Berkeley in that its plot concerned a company of marines stationed in Hawaii and thus provided the occasion for real military drills as well as 'high-brow jazz dancing'. The show consolidated Berkeley's reputation. (It also afforded him a role and the opportunity to introduce the show's hit song, 'You Took Advantage of Me'.) Reviews cite the 'whirlwind pace' of a chorus that met 'the tests of the eye and the stethoscope', the 'complicated and subtle rhythms that many a trained musician or trained artist dancer would find next to impossible to perform.'

Or, as the *New York Times* put it in July 1928 (around the time that Berkeley devised a ballet for *The Earl Carroll Vanities*, inspired by his visit to a Ford motor plant, and the same summer brought his 'mazes of syncopation' to the Salzburg Festival in Austria): 'Busby Berkeley assumes the mantle of a kind of modern prophet.'

II

I felt around Jack [Warner], and I think Harry [Warner], and I said, 'Don't you believe we're ready to go into a musical cycle again?' They said, 'Oh, Christ no, we can't give 'em away.'

Darryl F. Zanuck on the genesis of *42nd Street*, in Maurice Zolotow's *Don't Say Yes Until I Finish Talking* (1971).

42nd Street opens with a confidently upbeat blast of its martial theme and the most perfunctory of establishing shots – a wobbly aerial view of midtown Manhattan. This shaky swoop over the skyline becomes a crude city symphony – a montage of street corners that, accompanied by honking car horns and the rumble of the elevated, hops crazily along 42nd Street from Vanderbilt Avenue west to Eighth and Ninth Avenues, rebounding east to Sixth, Fifth, Lexington and Third Avenues, then finally back again to Times Square where the image dissolves into a low-angle shot of a theatrical agent urgently jabbering on the phone that 'Jones and Barry are doing a show!'

'Jones and Barry are doing a show!' Hysteria mounts as additional show business types – a would-be chorine, a drama desk reporter, a sugar daddy and his date perched upon a divan – receive and pass on the exciting message. Lips are shown in gigantic, screen-filling close-up. Multiple faces are dancingly superimposed, the dialogue madly overlaps. Even telephone linemen are drawn into the proceedings ('testing, testing'), not to mention the magnificently jaded operator who, informed that 'Jones and Barry are doing a show', bats her eyes and drawls, 'You're telling me?'

Yes, 'Jones and Barry are doing a show!' *42nd Street* immediately announces itself as a newsworthy spectacle. But of course, from *The Jazz Singer* on, the American movie musical has been characteristically and self-reflexively an entertainment about entertainment, a show about show business, or a demonstration of its own capabilities. And, thanks to *The Jazz Singer* too, the movie musical was for a time the quintessential talking picture.

American studios released sixty movie musicals in 1928. By May 1929, one in four films in production was a musical – most devoted to some aspect of the theatre, vaudeville, burlesque, nightclubs or minstrel shows. In this, the movies were following Broadway's lead and chasing their own tail: Rick Altman suggests that legitimate theatre responded to the Hollywood star-system with a series of 'backstage' dramas. The first of many, Avery Hopwood's *The Gold Diggers*, produced by David Belasco in 1919, was entirely set in the apartment of three aspiring chorines.

Providing 'the illusion of seeing something which theatergoers cannot perceive', as Altman notes, the backstage movie is a more literal exposé. 'The theater audience's gaze is stopped by the stage backdrop, but the film audience can see right through that backdrop and into the wings.' Compounding 'legitimate' voyeurism, the strategy linking glamorous onstage entertainment to sordid backstage intrigue was initiated with MGM's first sound film, *The Broadway Melody*, which opened in February 1929, hailed by the *New York Times* as 'teeming with the vernacular of the bright lights and back-stage argot'; it was seconded later that year by Warners' two-strip Technicolor *On with the Show*. (Both films have been offered as sources for *42nd Street*: *The Broadway Melody* reeks of atmosphere, even featuring, as *42nd Street* would, its songwriters in cameo parts, while the climax of *On with the*

 'Jones and Barry are doing a show!'

Show has a humble hat-check girl replace a star who refuses to play her last scene.)

The bottom fell out of the musical market in 1930, a year when more than seventy musicals were released, including the disastrous *Glorifying the American Girl*. It was not simply that, as Ethan Mordden has written, 'Hollywood had churned out too many shapeless musicals without tempo or grade' (although that was assuredly so). *Whoopee!*, for example, was promoted as a genuine $6.60 Broadway production and *Photoplay* rhapsodised that it was superior to the original.

> It's Sam Goldwyn at his best, Flo Ziegfeld at his best. You can't beat a team like that. Don't say you're fed up on musical comedies. Go to see *Whoopee!* instead. The million and a half spent on it is justified. ... This is the new type of screen musical. There is no attempt at realism. It's simply a rollicking, roistering, beautiful production that will make you forget Hoover's advice to sit tight because better times are coming. Heck! They are here!

But while *Whoopee!* was a smash in New York and the other, mainly northern, cities where Ziegfeld companies regularly toured, the talkies themselves were not universally appreciated, especially when they trafficked in urban 'sophistication' and particularly in the hinterlands where audiences might resent the Broadway sharpies who had displaced their favourite stars. The inchoate 'New Deal in Entertainment' which *Whoopee!* seemed to presage (for *Photoplay* at least) was still over two years away.

By 1931, Warners felt compelled to cut their losses by dropping the Cole Porter songs from *Fifty Million Frenchmen* (1931), a show that the studio itself had backed on Broadway. Indeed, the only successful musicals of the 1931–2 season were Paramount's *The Big Broadcast*, a vehicle for crooner Bing Crosby which also featured radio star Kate Smith, and its 'boudoir' operettas – *The Love Parade*, *Monte Carlo*, *One Hour With You*, *Love Me Tonight*, mainly starring Maurice Chevalier and mostly directed by Ernst Lubitsch – and Goldwyn's two Eddie Cantor films, *Whoopee!* and *Palmy Days*.

On 22 July 1932 Florenz Ziegfeld died in Hollywood, a million dollars in debt. Between the 1927 and 1931 *Follies*, Ziegfeld had lost his fortune and suffered three successive flops, as well as all manner of

Auditioning: (l. to r.) Busby Berkeley, Darryl Zanuck, Mervyn LeRoy and associate executive Raymond Griffith

physical and mental illnesses. But a few weeks after Ziegfeld expired, Warner Bros' ambitious 30-year-old production chief Darryl F. Zanuck set out to extend the Ziegfeld legacy by other, industrial, means.

In a two-part profile, *The New Yorker* celebrated Zanuck as 'a great journalist'. Zanuck was 'the chief interpreter of the Hardboiled Era' which he had initiated in late 1930 with the aptly titled *Doorway to Hell*, 'a cold and gory picture' without a happy ending, a hero, or a sympathetic character: 'The Warners regarded it as a reckless experiment and allowed Zanuck to spend only a small sum in making it, but it was a box-office hit.' This first gangster film, arriving the year the musical genre fell apart, was followed in April 1931 by 'Zanuck's masterpiece', *The Public Enemy*, and ultimately by a whole gangster cycle.

Now, once more ahead of the curve, Zanuck proposed to revive the musical and replace the percussive sound of machine-gun fire with that of tap-dancing – paying a 28-year-old ex-vaudeville dancer named Bradford Ropes $6,000 for the rights to his forthcoming novel *42nd Street*, a backstage potboiler divided into two parts, 'Rehearsal' and 'Opening', and concerned with the interlocking fates of a show's producers and principals. Deeming *42nd Street* 'excessively vulgar' and 'gossipy' and definitely 'not a book to give to a maiden aunt', the *New York Times* reviewer nevertheless detected 'the sure touch of a writer thoroughly at home with his theme'.

In *42nd Street*, then, Zanuck concocted the Hardboiled Musical, imbued – like his gangster films – with what Baudelaire termed the 'Heroism of Modern Life', those 'thousands of floating existences – criminals and kept women – that drift about in the underworlds of a great city.' (So, too, the Great Ziegfeld, who had turned to mobster Dutch Schultz to finance his last fiasco, *Hot-Cha*.)

'Jones and Barry are doing a show!' Taking scarcely more than half a minute, this introduction transmits the equivalent of an all-points alert to the possibility that someone is actually hiring. By 1932, after all, one-third of the nation's labour force was unemployed. Four-fifths of the steel mills were closed. Farm income was a third of what it had been in 1929. Even Warner Bros, which as the pioneer talkie purveyor was initially immunised to the Depression, was facing losses of nearly $14,000,000.

The work motif continues with the first narrative gambit, a close-up of an Equity contract belonging to one Dorothy Brock. 'Well, of course I'm not a lawyer, I'm in the kiddie car business,' exclaims the pumpkin-faced Abner Dillon (Guy Kibbee), an infantile industrialist capable of crashing the economy all by himself. 'But – it looks good to me.' Following his train of thought, the camera pans across to close in on a pair of legs presumably belonging to Brock, then cuts to a *New Yorker* cover with the actress (Bebe Daniels) peering coyly over the top.

Not only an object for sale, fragmented in a manner to suggest a Surrealist photograph, Brock is also dressed to make an impression. Elegantly turned out in a tiara and evening clothes, she's initially quite gracious given Dillon's hapless creepiness, thanking him for helping her find a vehicle in 'this Depression' as she hands him his hat. When the would-be sugar daddy reveals that 'I'd like to do something for you – if you'd do something for me', Brock feigns a confusion that barely covers her annoyance. She is, however, a realist. But as the side deal appears to be taking shape with a close-up of the ardent Dillon, there's a dissolve to the Jones and Barry office where the as yet unseen Julian Marsh (Warner Baxter) is signing his contract.

The show, *Pretty Lady*, which is the subject of *42nd Street* (as well as the object of Abner Dillon's desire), is introduced first as an employment opportunity and then as a series of economic agreements, with Brock's devalued status reinforced by Marsh's unimpressed opening line that 'These days, stars like Dorothy Brock are a dime a dozen.' Even more than Dillon, Jones (Robert McWade) and Barry (Ned Sparks) are eager to flaunt their investment: 'That's why we got you, Julian – Julian Marsh,' the name comes rolling off Barry's tongue, 'the greatest musical comedy director in America today.'

Thus *42nd Street*'s two nominal stars, Warner Baxter and Bebe Daniels, are designated contract employees, lucky even to have a job. Perhaps they truly felt that way – both were silent movie performers who had successfully made the transition to sound. Baxter, then 41, was a loan-out from Fox (paid $31,200 for six weeks) who broke into movies at the close of the First World War and eased into sound as the star of 'the first outdoor talkie', *In Old Arizona* (1929), taking the part of O. Henry's 'lovable bandit' by default after the intended leading man, Raoul Walsh, lost an eye in an automobile accident; he won an Oscar and reprised the role in *The Cisco Kid* (1931). Daniels, 31, was a former child actress who had worked for Hal Roach and Cecil B. DeMille and, primarily a comedienne, appeared opposite Harold Lloyd and Rudolph Valentino. Paramount let her go with the arrival of sound; she moved to the newly constituted RKO, scored a personal triumph in the 1929 Ziegfeld adaptation *Rio Rita*, made four more pictures and went on to United Artists to co-star with Douglas Fairbanks in *Reaching for the Moon* (1931), an Irving Berlin musical in which all musical numbers, save one, were cut. Currently working under a six-picture deal with Warners, Daniels was most often cast as a woman of experience, best remembered in the Mary Astor role opposite Ricardo Cortez's Humphrey Bogart in the first, 1931 version of *The Maltese Falcon*.

More topically, Guy Kibbee had most recently appeared in *The Dark Horse*, Warners' contribution to election year entertainment. Kibbee portrayed a candidate for governor, managed by a fast-talking political operative (Warren William), and 'so dumb that every time he opens his mouth he subtracts from the sum total of human knowledge.' The Kibbee character was explicitly compared to former president Calvin Coolidge – posing in an Indian headdress, pretending to go trout fishing, trained to answer every question with 'Yes and then again, no.' He also handily won election, justifying his manager's strategy: 'We're going to convince the voters that they're getting one of them. That's what [they] want in these days of corruption and Depression.'

And speaking of Depression, Marsh (who was originally to be played by Warren William) is busy pulling on a cigarette and barking like a dog at his new employers: 'I'm in this for one reason only – money.' The partners, Jones and Barry, seem unduly puzzled. 'Say,' Marsh asks, 'did you ever hear of Wall Street?' And there it is again … the Great Crash. Suddenly, a telephone call from Marsh's doctor. Jones and Barry don't hear just what this chain-smoking lunatic is told ('Good Lord, man, you're not a machine – that body of yours will only stand so much'), but they don't need to; they've remembered that, no less than the American economy, their new director had suffered a nervous breakdown. (Although it is clear in the context of *42nd Street* that Marsh is a Ziegfeld figure, Baxter is also a fitting emblem of the Roaring Twenties, having played the title role in the 1926 version of *The Great Gatsby*.)

Anxious consternation, with the partners stepping on each other's lines. 'You'll get your *Pretty Lady*,' Marsh assures them, gazing out of the office window at the (unseen) street – the 'gulch down there' that's 'taken everything I've had to offer' and paid off 'in money I couldn't hang on to'. Then Marsh starts to soliloquise, spitting out a machine-gun elegy for the 20s: 'Fair-weather friends, women, headlines! Why even the cops and newsboys recognise me on sight ... Marsh the Magnificent, Marsh the Slave-Driver! Actors tell you how I drove 'em and bullied 'em and even tore it out of them!' Marsh softens his tone slightly: 'And maybe a few'll tell you how Marsh really made 'em.' Now he's shouting again that 'they all have something to show for it ... except Marsh! Well, this is my last shot!' After this show, he yells, he'll sock his money away so hard they (whoever they are) will need dynamite to blast it loose.

Before he departs, Marsh warns Jones and Barry that he's going to be 'Boss with a capital B', reinforcing the idea that *42nd Street* is a movie with a surplus of bosses: Harry Warner, Sam Warner, Darryl F. Zanuck, director Lloyd Bacon, dance director Busby Berkeley, and Marsh himself – not to mention the ghostly figure of Franklin D. Roosevelt. As the 1932 election neared, there was considerable demand for 'strong' leadership. That spring, Senator David A. Reed of Pennsylvania had observed that 'if this country ever needed a Mussolini, it needs one now.' A few months later, on the eve of the Democratic Convention, *Vanity Fair* cried out that the nation should 'appoint a dictator!', while *Liberty* called for 'martial law' and a president with 'dictatorial powers'.

Summer releases included Frank Capra's *American Madness* – Walter Huston playing a version of populist banker A.P. Giannini, 'swell propaganda against hoarding, frozen assets and other economic evils which 1932 Hooverism has created,' according to *Variety* – and MGM's *The Washington Masquerade*, with Lionel Barrymore as a newly elected reform senator who unsuccessfully battles the monopolies. Despite the appropriation of Roosevelt's 'forgotten man', the protagonist of a celebrated radio speech made in April on behalf of the Democratic National Committee, *The Washington Masquerade* was, like MGM studio boss Louis B. Mayer, staunchly pro-Hoover: Barrymore blames a corrupt Congress for the economic mess and dies citing 'a man in the White House whose heart is broken because we're traitors'.

The Dark Horse opened that fall, along with Paramount's *The Phantom President*, in which a dull candidate is replaced by his *doppelgänger*, a smooth snake-oil salesman (George M. Cohan in his movie debut), and Columbia's *Washington Merry-Go-Round*. Here too, a newly elected reformer finds the Congress dominated by vested interests and cynical lobbyists. 'Never in the history of this country has there been a greater opportunity for a strong man,' one scoundrel declares. 'Italy has her Mussolini, Russia her Stalin. Such a man will arise in America too.'

Darryl Zanuck had no political ambitions but, like the hero of *The Last Tycoon*, he was one of the few in Hollywood who kept the whole equation of pictures in his head. He assigned Whitney Bolton to adapt the Ropes novel and created the team of Al Dubin and Harry Warren, both established Tin Pan Alley tunesmiths, to produce a score. Dubin, one of the first lyricists to go to Hollywood, was already under contract to Warners; Harry Warren (born Salvatore Guaragna) was a former song-plugger who had played the piano in Brooklyn movie-houses, as well as for Corrine Griffith on the Vitagraph set, and had been 'acquired' when Warners bought the Remick Music Company. Hired at $1,500 each per week, the new team was brought to Burbank. Warren remembers the Warners studio as a desert: 'You looked out the window, and you couldn't see anything. And hotter than hell. ... No air conditioning.' Although they were given proofs of the novel to read, Warren and Dubin were told to write the score as a revue rather than a book show. Warren imagined that the screenplay was actually written after the music, which is entirely possible.

On 16 August, Bolton delivered a 38-page treatment; for the next month, he and James Seymour (the Harvard-educated son of a British stage director) worked on the screenplay. They retained the basic plot – the innocent Peggy Sawyer, originally the daughter of a minister, becomes the star of *Pretty Lady* after the leading lady Dorothy Brock is injured just before opening night – and kept some of the tawdry details, like director Julian Marsh using a gangster to break up the romance between Brock and Pat Denning to ensure that Brock will devote herself to the show's angel. But although the Bolton treatment echoes the novel, ending with Sawyer staring into the mirror, a prematurely disillusioned success, the screenplay generally softens Ropes's characterisations. Marsh, an English homosexual who is keeping Billy Lawler, is neutered; the opportunist angel transformed into Abner Dillon; the womanising dance director rendered essentially harmless. In general, Marsh's role is contracted as Sawyer's expands and she's paired with Billy Lawler for the clinch – although it is now the rival chorus girl Ann, and not the juvenile Lawler, who gives Sawyer her chance.

After a rewrite in which Marsh was effectively Ziegfeldised (transformed into a broke American), Bolton was dropped and at the last possible moment Rian James, signed by Warners in July, was taken off *The Mind Reader* and brought in for what *Variety* called 'a three-day rush revise'. James, 32, personified the Warners world view. A columnist for seven years on the *Brooklyn Daily Eagle*, he had been a foreign correspondent, a parachute jumper, a stunt man, an airmail pilot, and a vaudeville actor. (His novel *Love is a Racket*, a hardboiled account of newshounds and gangsters mixing it on Broadway, was the basis for William Wellman's movie, released by First National in June 1932.) James improved the dialogue with slangy wisecracks and topical references; his revise also beefed up the most famous scene (Brock's arrival on crutches, Marsh's climactic pep-talk).

On 8 September, Warners announced that *42nd Street* would go into production with an 'all-star cast' that included Warren William, Kay Francis, Joan Blondell and Glenda Farrell. (None of them wound up in the picture, but the substitutions are revealing of Warners' assembly-line *typage*: William replaced by Baxter, Francis by Daniels, Blondell by Ginger Rogers, and Farrell by Una Merkel.) By the time Ropes's novel was published in mid-September, fifty-seven girls had been hired at $66 per week and the 37-year-old Busby Berkeley signed to direct the dances for the 'partly musical' *42nd Street*.

The idea of bringing in Berkeley was Mervyn LeRoy's. After completing the dances for *Whoopee!*, Berkeley had been hired by Paramount but got no work. He returned to New York, then went back to California to direct the dances for an unreleased Mary Pickford film and for Goldwyn's next Cantor vehicle, *Palmy Days*. LeRoy, who (uncredited) directed a few scenes of *Palmy Days*, advised Berkeley to stay put in Hollywood; musicals would surely come back. (Again prematurely, *Photoplay* agreed: 'Ten-to-one [*Palmy Days*] will bring back film musicals in a veritable inundation. It's THAT good!')

While waiting, Berkeley went to work for the Los Angeles agency Fanchon and Marco, which specialised in producing stage prologues for first-run movie theatres (thus providing the inspiration for *Footlight Parade*). He also directed the dances for MGM's *Flying High*, deploying dancers in quasi-military formations filmed, according to *Photoplay*, from 'weird angles'; for Universal's *Night World*; and for RKO's Polynesian romance, *Bird of Paradise*. When *Palmy Days*, which opened in September 1931, went on to gross over a million dollars, Goldwyn borrowed as much from the Bank of America to make *The Kid from Spain*, another Cantor vehicle that was a blatant steal from Ziegfeld's swan-song *Hot-Cha*. Berkeley had just finished directing the numbers when he was signed by Warners at $1,750 per week.

LeRoy helped to prepare *42nd Street*, but was too exhausted to begin work on it. (He directed six features in 1932, including *I am a Fugitive from a Chain Gang*.) Zanuck replaced him with another Warners workhorse, Lloyd Bacon. Son of comedian Frank Bacon, star and writer of *Lightnin'*, the first Broadway production to run for 1,000 performances, the 43-year-old director had acted, as a youth, with Broncho Billy Anderson and Charlie Chaplin; he directed comedy shorts for Mack Sennett and was employed by First National when Warners bought the company in the late 20s.

Between 1927 and 1929, Bacon made fourteen films, including Warners' all-time money-maker *The Singing Fool* (1928); the 1930 *Moby Dick* (a happy version in which Ahab kills the whale and returns to New Bedford); the non-music musical *Fifty Million Frenchmen*; the Technicolor backstage comedy *Manhattan Parade* (1931); and, one of his six films released in 1932, the radio musical *Crooner*, from a script by Rian James. Bacon had a reputation as a fast worker. He was technically rather bland, at least as compared to his Warners colleagues, but he was supposedly Jack Warner's favourite and, with a salary of $4,225 per week (only $775 less than Zanuck's), the studio's highest paid director. *42nd Street* is not even mentioned among the ten films cited in his *New York Times* obituary.

Production began on 28 September 1932 at a time when Jack Warner was preoccupied with another spectacle. Warner was chairman

Overleaf: Lloyd Bacon directs (extreme left). Listening (l. to r.) are George Brent, Warner Baxter, Ned Sparks, Bebe Daniels, Allen Jenkins, Eddie Nugent, Ruby Keeler, Una Merkel, George E. Stone, Robert McWade, Ginger Rogers, Guy Kibbee, Dick Powell

of the motion picture division of the Democratic campaign and, when Franklin Roosevelt swung west in late September, was asked to produce a suitable pageant. Having already contributed $50,000 to the Roosevelt campaign, Warner organised a Saturday afternoon rally at the Hollywood Bowl on 24 September, with Roosevelt asking the people of the United States 'to stand for a new deal'. This was followed by an evening 'electrical parade' and polo display at the Los Angeles Coliseum with Roosevelt as guest of honour. *42nd Street* stars Warner Baxter and Bebe Daniels were both present while, by enlisting Marion Davies as co-sponsor (half the receipts going to her charitable foundation), Warner reaped maximum Hearst publicity. The crowd was put at 65,000, although *Variety* noted that prominent Hollywood Republicans were conspicuous by their absence; *The Phantom President* opened in Los Angeles the next day.

Warner's outside interests may have served Zanuck's purposes. Nearly forty years later, he would explain to his biographer Maurice Zolotow that he decided to shoot *42nd Street*'s musical numbers without Warner's knowledge. According to the legend, Zanuck had two movies in simultaneous production – a backstage melodrama directed by Bacon at First National and a musical shot by Berkeley at the old Vitagraph studio, supposedly at night. (In fact, the two 'movies' were shot consecutively. The Bacon unit occupied six sound-stages until 29 October, with two days of retakes on 2 and 3 November; the Berkeley unit was in production for eighteen days, including five days rehearsing the title number, which was shot from 12–15 November. Sol Polito, moreover, is the only credited cameraman.)

According to Zanuck, when he and Bacon combined the footage, they hedged their bets by backloading the musical numbers – if necessary they could be cut without impeding the narrative. 'Then,' Zanuck told Zolotow, 'the time came when we had to screen the picture.'

> Jack went out of his mind. He never knew until it was screened that it was a musical. Only one thing, he loved it! He said, 'What am I going to tell Harry? Do you have another version?' But he sent the musical version to Harry in New York and Harry wired back 'This is the greatest picture you've sent me in five years.'

But Zanuck's account is clearly exaggerated. For one thing, at $379,000, *42nd Street* was relatively lavish (50 per cent more than the average Warners production). For another, the 8 November issue of *Variety*, published in the midst of Berkeley's shoot, announced that 'Harry Warner picked *42nd Street* as a special after seeing but six reels.'

On 9 November 1932 (two days before the opening of *I am a Fugitive from a Chain Gang*), Roosevelt defeated Hoover. Los Angeles county went for the Democrats for the first time since 1916; *Variety* speculated that Jack Warner would have the same relationship with the new president that Louis B. Mayer enjoyed with Hoover. Within a week, Zanuck began pre-production on a second musical, a remake of Warners' 1929 *Gold Diggers of Broadway*. James Seymour's treatment was submitted at the end of the month under the temporary title *High Life*. Meanwhile pre-release publicity for *42nd Street* continued. An article bearing Zanuck's name appeared in December in the *Hollywood Reporter* announcing that

> We have just completed a musical exposé, *Forty-second Street* [sic], which dramatically endeavors to lift the curtain and reveal the strenuous, heartbreaking efforts of a well known Broadway producer to stage a musical comedy in this year of depression.

That year was coming to a dismal conclusion. On 5 December, a double line of police, armed with tear gas and riot guns, blocked the steps of the Capitol against 1,200 Communist hunger marchers. While Frank Capra was at work at MGM on *Soviet*, a supposedly sympathetic treatment of contemporary Russian life (cancelled by Mayer after Irving Thalberg's Christmas Day heart attack), Warners promised another sort of attraction: 'More sex is going to come out of the Warner–First National studio from now on,' *Variety* predicted.

The movie industry was felt to be near collapse. Theatres were empty, production was down, investment capital and cash flow had dried up. In mid-December, Warner Bros's annual stockholders meeting attracted so large a turnout it had to be relocated to a nearby movie theatre. The Warners withstood a heated proxy battle, defeating an attempt to investigate their finances as well as a putative takeover bid by DuPont. It was not simply that the studio was losing money; it was compelled to choose between paying upwards of a million dollars in interest or, like Paramount and RKO, going into receivership. In late December, *Variety* reported that Warners had determined to reduce costs even further by putting the average budget below $200,000, doubling up on extras, cutting down on retakes and instituting a new 18-day shooting schedule. The studio hoped to complete forty-five features by April, then shut down production for the summer. *42nd Street* was one of nineteen unreleased features, representing an investment of $4 million and contributing to the studio's cash-flow problem. A series of successful sneak previews held in early January 1933, however, encouraged Warners to go for broke.

Exhibitors were instructed to sell *42nd Street* as 'the Biggest Screen Event since the Birth of Vitaphone'. The film's trailer announces that 'out in Hollywood the sensation of the moment is the picture *42nd Street* ... the drama of the production behind a big Broadway musical from the rehearsals to the grand finale', with 'amazing chorus ensembles, lavish settings, spectacular dance routines', and 'scenes never before attempted on stage and screen'. Warner Bros, 'who gave you *Golddiggers of Broadway*, *The Jazz Singer*, and *The Singing Fool*, surpass these great hits with *42nd Street* – another milestone in the art of talking pictures.'

Distilling Berkeley's 'Young and Healthy' into a few frenzied minutes, the trailer flashes a kaleidoscope of faces, a pinwheel of thighs, and series of rotating silhouettes that suggest a nineteenth-century zoetrope. Clearly 'Young and Healthy' was perceived as a potential money scene. The January 1933 issue of *Photoplay* touted the three revolving turntables used in the sequence as something unique, explaining that cameras were mounted at the periphery of these round stages and thus travel with it: 'As the dancers go through their movements, the effect is dizzying and breath-taking – one finds himself gripping the seat ahead for support.' (A picture of Berkeley directing the sequence is included, although he is unidentified.)

The chorine-filled rotating stage, something Ziegfeld had introduced as early as 1906, had particular significance for Berkeley. In *The Kid from Spain*, completed just before *42nd Street*, he directed a cabaret scene in which chorus girls performed on huge, circular, two-tiered pedestals. 'One day I asked Goldwyn, "Can I make these things revolve?" He said, "No, I don't want them to revolve. Do it the way it is now and if you must revolve them, do that at some other studio."' Berkeley took Goldwyn's advice and requested the turntables for the 'Young and Healthy' number in *42nd Street*. He was filming them when Zanuck visited the set.

> I staged this number with three revolving platforms, and I explained to Zanuck that I couldn't show him exactly what he would see on the screen because I planned to shoot in cuts. I outlined the continuity for him and showed him my camera placements, then had Dick Powell and the boys and girls go through the number in sections. Zanuck and the others seemed very pleased with the performance and the staging I had planned; he turned to the executives who were with him and said, 'Give Berkeley whatever he wants in the way of sets, props, costumes. Anything he wants, he can have.'

Although the *Los Angeles Times* had already publicised the open beauty contests Berkeley held to pick the chorus for what was still being called *High Life*, Jack Warner waited until the end of January to announce that *42nd Street* would be followed by another musical. (Typically, Warner stressed that no further musicals were scheduled. Nevertheless, *Film Daily* predicted that with Warners leading the way 'the success of *42nd Street* will probably bring a new avalanche of musicals.')

Angling for an opening at RKO's new Radio City Music Hall and manoeuvring for national promotion on the NBC radio network, Warners courted General Electric, RKO and NBC's corporate parent. The studio chartered a train, embellished the outside with gold leaf, equipped the cars with futuristic GE appliances – including an 'Electric Health Kitchen', a 'Portable Broadcast Station', and a 'Miniature Malibu Beach' created with sunlamps – and filled the berths with Warners contractees. The train was called the '42nd Street Special'. An electric sign bore the message 'Better Times'.

Better Times. In January 1933, the month that Adolf Hitler came to power in Germany, Farrar and Rinehart published an anonymous novel entitled *Gabriel Over the White House*. Set in the late 1930s, with the Depression having worsened, the book describes the presidency of Judson Hammond, a party hack who is transformed into a political messiah in the aftermath of a near-fatal car crash.

Gabriel Over the White House was written by Thomas F. Tweed, once Lloyd George's political secretary, with revisions by *Time*'s Washington correspondent John Billings. Tweed claimed to have been inspired by statements to the effect that what the US needed was a 'benign dictator'. Indeed, the cult of direct action continued to grow. Political columnist Walter Lippman urged president-elect Roosevelt to 'assume virtually dictatorial powers in dealing with the crisis' and his recommendation was echoed across the political spectrum. Roosevelt's former Democratic rival Al Smith and his future Republican rival Alf Landon both announced the need for an American strongman. While the Socialist leader Norman Thomas warned of a trend towards 'an American brand of fascist dictatorship', the business journal *Barron's* confessed that 'sometimes openly, and at other times secretly, we have been longing to see the superman emerge.'

More sinister forces coalesced – self-proclaimed Minute Men and the openly fascist Silver Shirts. At least one religious publication saw apocalyptic portents in the winter's events: according to biblical prophecy, the final tribulations might be on hand. On 16 February, the day after the president-elect narrowly escaped an assassination attempt, an event suitably dramatised in Fox's *The Man Who Dared*, released the following September, Mervyn LeRoy began production on what was now called *The Gold Diggers of 1933*. (In addition to dances by Berkeley, a script by James Seymour, and a score by Warren and Dubin, the cast was heavily drawn from *42nd Street*: Ruby Keeler, Dick Powell, Ginger Rogers, Guy Kibbee and Ned Sparks, plus Joan Blondell and Warren William.) The next week, the '42nd Street Special' left Hollywood 'on the greatest ride since Paul Revere', carrying 'news of a Revolution in Picture Art!' and 'leaving a trail of millions of ticket buyers for WARNER BROS. NEW DEAL IN ENTERTAINMENT'.

According to *Variety*, *42nd Street* was the first studio release to be given extensive playdates in the American heartland, before opening in either New York or Los Angeles. The world premiere was on 23 February in Denver, where the '42nd Street Special' was met by the governor of Colorado and 'business was practically suspended.' The next day, in Kansas City, *42nd Street* opened in 'a blaze of glory' and 'the hottest of circus publicity'. The mayor was on hand and 'streets were jammed for several hours while the mob waited for the celebrities.'

The '42nd Street Special' stopped in Chicago on 25 February, then made its way through Cleveland, Toledo and Memphis. On 3 March, there was a panicky, pre-inaugural run on the nation's banks. The next day the Special arrived in Washington D.C. Never before had Hollywood been represented in a presidential procession: eleven movie stars and twelve chorus girls took part, occupying a float of their own. Monday 6 March (the day Busby Berkeley began shooting the numbers for *Gold Diggers of 1933*), Roosevelt proclaimed a 'bank holiday', which would negatively affect *42nd Street*'s Baltimore opening.

Finally, on 9 March, the '42nd Street Special' – carrying Warners stars Tom Mix, Joe E. Brown, Bette Davis, Preston Foster, Leo Carrillo and Laura LaPlante, not to mention Olympic swimming champion Eleanor Holm, a number of chorines, and a stowaway named Doris McMahon – arrived at Grand Central Station in time to mark the 108th anniversary of the deeding of 42nd Street to the city of New York with a gala lunch at the nearby Hotel Commodore. 'If the gods had descended on Manhattan, there couldn't have been more excitement,' *Photoplay* reported.

42nd Street had already been shown the previous evening to benefit the Service League of the New York State Division of the Women's Organization for National Prohibition Reform, raising funds to repeal the 18th Amendment; that morning, the movie was unveiled for the public at the Strand, the 2,758-seat theatre on Broadway between 48th and 49th Streets which was then Warners' flagship venue. The doors opened early at 9 a.m. and an extra show was added after midnight. Outside, winds of up to fifty miles an hour lashed the city, breaking windows and downing trees.

She Done Him Wrong was at the Rialto, *The Kid from Spain* at Loew's State. *King Kong* completed its second week at the Roxy *and* Radio City, while a rival mass spectacle, *Soviet Parade*, was at the RKO Cameo where posters were emblazoned: 'Cast: 160,000,000. Locale: One Sixth of the World. Stars: Stalin, Gorky, Red Army.' Still, the 14 March *Variety* reported Broadway 'blah' except for *42nd Street*, which grossed $40,000, and *Mussolini Speaks*, a documentary released by Columbia on the recommendation of director Frank Capra and banker A.H. Giannini, which (advertised with the question, 'Is this what America needs?') brought in $12,000.

III

> Not only were they American products; at the same time they demonstrated the greatness of American production. ... When they formed an undulating snake, they radiantly illustrated the virtues of the conveyor belt; when they tapped their feet in fast tempo, it sounded like *business, business*; when they kicked their legs high with mathematical precision, they joyously affirmed the progress of rationalization; and when they kept repeating the same movements without ever interrupting their routine, one envisioned an uninterrupted chain of autos gliding from the factories of the world, and believed that the blessings of prosperity had no end.
>
> Siegfried Kracauer on the Tiller Girls, 'The Mass Ornament' (1927).

As the drama of *42nd Street* is largely predicated upon securing a job, so the spectacle of the movie is most often 'work'. The casting call for *Pretty Lady* is treated as a newsworthy event, the camera sweeping across a crowded stage or gazing down at the excited hubbub of prospective employees. Asked about the turnout, the officiously gum-chewing stage-manager MacElroy (Allen Jenkins, a specialist in bumbling tough guys) calls it 'fifty-fifty – half are dumb and the other half dumber'. As Julian Marsh's henchman, MacElroy is matched in spurious authority by the diminutive dance director Andy Lee (another Warners contractee and frequent second-string gangster, George E. Stone). Lee is in charge of selecting the chorus, and as the hopeful Lorraine Fleming (Una Merkel), somewhat ridiculously turned out in a Tartan outfit, waves at him, the pained response that flits across his weak-chinned face suggests that there's something between them.

Lee nervously tells Lorraine that she's in, she's set – 'now scram!' – and, turning to flee, slams into the even loonier-looking Ann Lowell (Ginger Rogers). Clutching her pet Pekinese and squinting through a monocle as though trying to pass herself off as a slumming aristocrat, Ann affects an imperious drawl. Still, sprightly Lorraine has little difficulty recognising her: 'Come out from under that accent, Ann!' Neither does Andy, who leers: 'Not "Anytime Annie"? Say, who could forget her? She only said "no" once, and then she didn't hear the question!' (This is one of the few risqué remarks retained from the novel. 'Gee, you been abroad?' Lorraine then asks, in a tasty bit of pre-Code punning.)

The prospects line up to display their charms, offering further diversion by slinging slangy one-liners. Suddenly, the confused Peggy Sawyer (Ruby Keeler) appears from behind a piano. This genteel innocent, instantly named 'dearie', is raw meat for the tough chorines. 'You looking for someone – or just shopping around?' one asks. They send her first into the men's toilet, then into the dressing-room of the goofy Billy Lawler (Dick Powell). Sawyer responds to this hazing with acute embarrassment, shielding her eyes, cringing away from the sight of Lawler in his underwear. Totally unabashed, he introduces himself as 'one of Broadway's better juveniles'. 'Oh, I thought you were someone important,' she whines, articulating the movie's own point of view. Powell, then 28, had been an MC in Louisville, a band-singer in Indianapolis and a radio star in Pittsburgh before he was signed by Warners at $500 a week to play crooner-stooge to Lee Tracy's Winchellesque radio reporter in the 1932 *Blessed Event*. *42nd Street* was Powell's fourth film – he would appear in five other 1933 releases – and

Ginger Rogers with monocle and George E. Stone

his weekly salary had fallen to $98.

Lawler and Sawyer chat for a bit, mainly about Sawyer's lack of experience – ironically, considering Keeler's real-life résumé – and together exit his dressing-room to run the gauntlet of dirty-minded chorines. 'Well, if it isn't Little Lord Fauntleroy and the village maiden,' one cracks. 'Made in New York and all points west,' another unseen wiseacre ripostes. The self-important Lawler tells MacElroy he's taking Sawyer to see Marsh ('That'll just about make Marsh's day perfect' is MacElroy's observation) but winds up simply pushing the wide-eyed girl in the great man's direction. 'Quit shoving,' some hardboiled cookie drawls as Sawyer lurches through the line. Jostled by this newcomer, Lorraine looks over at her pal Ann and, in a magnificent gesture, shakes her head while letting her jaw drop – signifying Sawyer as an idiot.

By then Ruby Keeler was something of professional naif. The 23-year-old dancer grew up on the East Side of Manhattan and was performing in speakeasies by her early teens, consistently attracting the attention of powerful men. Both Florenz Ziegfeld and Al Jolson saw Keeler dance at the well-known nightspot run by Texas Guinan (who would subsequently play herself in Warners' 1929 *Queen of the Nightclubs*). Jolson wooed Keeler away from her gangster protector, Johnny 'Irish' Costello; Ziegfeld cast her in the 1928 stage production of *Whoopee!*, although when the 43-year-old Jolson married the 19-year-old Keeler in September 1928, he demanded that she drop out of the cast and accompany him to California.

Keeler had already appeared in a two-minute short made by Fox to test the sound quality of recorded tap-dancing. 'Ruby Keeler, a revue dancer, snapped through a short but nifty tap-dance,' *Variety* reported. 'The machine gets every tap and reveals Miss Keeler as an exceptional female hoofer.' In Hollywood, she was immediately offered a part opposite Jolson but declined ('Al is so nervous when he works'), returning to New York in the spring of 1929 to star in another Ziegfeld-produced vehicle, *Show Girl*. This time Jolson followed her, and his initially extemporaneous gimmick of singing to his wife from the audience gave the production a needed boost. Unfortunately, Keeler's run was cut short after she fell from a spiral staircase and broke her ankle. Back in Hollywood, Joseph Schenk had her screen-tested for the female lead in the Jolson vehicle *Hallelujah I'm a Bum*. The powers at

Warners saw the test and, despite a report in the *Los Angeles Times* that Jolson 'hasn't been exactly keen over the idea of his wife entering on a motion picture career', offered her a leading part in *42nd Street*. Negotiating with the studio he had helped propel to solvency, Jolson demanded $10,000 for Keeler and got it. Keeler, in turn, managed to obtain parts for her two sisters, Gertrude and Helen, in the chorus line.

At Marsh's command, the chorines lift their dresses in close-up to reveal their legs. (Watching the auditions from the audience, producer Barry turns to the over-excited angel Abner Dillon: 'Yeah, and they got pretty faces too.' Here in particular Ned Sparks's cold, unfocused stare and sepulchral bray suggest a skinny W.C. Fields.) Lorraine, who has inexplicably warmed to Sawyer – 'Stick with us, kid,' she advises – signals Andy to tell Marsh to take Sawyer too. 'Andy, you're a panic,' is Marsh's friendly response to the recommendation. 'I suppose if I don't keep them, you'll have to.'

This sequence, which introduces almost the entire supporting cast, offers a virtual taxonomy of American showbiz. The romantic leads, former radio crooner Dick Powell and upwardly mobile chorine Ruby Keeler, are surrounded by all manner of hopefuls and has-beens, youthful veterans and canny old-timers. The morose Ned Sparks, who had sung in Klondike honkytonks and barnstormed North America with countless road companies, showed a similar resourcefulness in expanding his role as the saturnine producer. (His memorably sour one-liners, delivered with an unlit cigar drooping from his lips, almost always rate a close-up.) Guy Kibbee, another roadshow veteran whose teeth gleam yellow even in black and white, had parlayed a bit as a lecherous sugar-daddy in the 1930 Broadway hit *Torch Song* into a Hollywood career playing variations on the theme. George E. Stone was a vaudeville song and dance kid who had been in movies since 1916. Ginger Rogers was a professional flapper who won a Charleston contest at 15, brought her bobbed hair and coy vocal delivery to Broadway, and then, a year into the Depression and barely out of her teens, left New York for Hollywood where she switched from baby-talking 'it' girl to wise-cracking gold-digger. She had just played a good-hearted chorine in the Fox production of *Broadway Bad* when Mervyn LeRoy, with whom she had been romantically involved, recommended her for *42nd Street*.

Rogers, of course, was to make it big the following year when RKO matched her with Broadway dancer Fred Astaire in *Flying Down to Rio*. But the sequence is stolen by Una Merkel, who thirty years later would get an Oscar nomination as Best Supporting Actress for her role in *Summer and Smoke*. Watching Merkel primp and flutter, double up her gestures and assume a different expression in each shot, all the while exaggerating her distinctively chirpy Southern drawl, it's not surprising to learn that this ironic performer was a trained and experienced stage actress who had also worked with D.W. Griffith, as a stand-in for Lillian Gish in *Way Down East* and *The White Rose* and then as Ann Rutledge in *Abraham Lincoln*. Nor was Merkel the only former Griffith star in the cast: Henry B. Walthall, who played The Little Colonel in *The Birth of a Nation*, was cast as an old actor who dies onstage during the dress rehearsal, a bit of show-must-go-on melodrama that never made it to the finished film.

The characters are mainly colourful urban types, despite their ethnic deracination. In the novel, which is replete with anti-Semitic slurs, Andy Lee is 'a product of the ghetto'; in the movie, he is played by – but not as – one. Similarly, the producers were transformed, in the

Ned Sparks (l.) and Guy Kibbee (centre) eye up the dancers *opposite*

final script, from the Jewish team of Friedman and Green to the neutral Jones and Barry. The corollary to the pervasive big city cynicism is the blatant (and titillating) sexual economics. If driven Julian Marsh is seemingly impervious to the charms of his co-workers, virtually everyone else in the show is either hustling or being hit on. Lorraine and Anytime Annie will do anything for a part. But when even the star Dorothy Brock is compelled to put out for the grotesque Abner Dillon, it's difficult to fault the sexual barter proposed by starving chorus girls – who are explicitly chosen for the attractiveness of their legs.

Ropes's novel, of course, is considerably more explicit than anything that even pre-Code Hollywood could consider: Marsh is infatuated with Billy Lawler, unemployed actor Pat Denning is sleeping not only with Dorothy Brock but also with the wife of dance director Andy Lee. Nevertheless, in its matter-of-fact acknowledgment of backstage prostitution, the movie *42nd Street* anticipates the less glamorous representation of '42nd Street' found in such post-Code films as John Schlesinger's 1968 *Midnight Cowboy* or Paul Morrissey's 1982 *Forty Deuce*. This tawdry backdrop makes the ludicrous innocence of Peggy Sawyer (and Billy Lawler) all the more dramatically

compelling – given the true nature of *Pretty Lady* (sic), the audience is left to wonder whether Sawyer will make it to the top with her virtue intact.

Sawyer becomes an issue once more when Andy Lee realises that they're missing something – he counts only thirty-nine girls. Marsh starts snarling but Lawler again saves Sawyer, pointing out that, although eliminated, she's still around, having fallen asleep behind a stage flat. Amid much laughter, Sawyer is woken up ('Hey you – with the legs – come out here') and, as if in a dream, accepted into the showbiz sorority. 'All right, get in line.' Of course, the youngster's telegraphed excitement as she scoots over with a big, overbright smile is subsumed by Marsh's characteristically dyspeptic pep talk. He paces up and down, glaring around the stage, brandishing his ubiquitous cigarette. 'You're gonna work and sweat and work some more,' he warns the company, promising them 'the toughest five weeks' they'll ever live through.

Despite the addition of Peggy Sawyer, *Pretty Lady* has its problems. The cast is walking through a leaden number called 'It Must Be June'. Distraction reigns: Lorraine is flirting with Andy Lee, MacElroy is blabbing away to some backstage crony. The star, Miss Brock, is rehearsing her lines. 'Things can never be the same now,' she sniffs, only to be corrected on some arcane point of intonation by the playwright (a character given so little respect that he has no name and the actor who plays him is not identified in the film's credits). They squabble, Marsh intervenes, and the scene ends with the line repeated, from the audience, by idiotic Abner. His self-satisfied delivery, as well as the killer look that Brock zaps him, suggests that by now they've probably had some sort of sex. Back in candyland, Billy Lawler drops in on Peggy Sawyer, who even rehearses in a puff-sleeved jumpsuit, but is aced out when his rival Terry (Eddie Nugent) cuts in to show the youngster 'that routine'.

The rest of the rehearsal is elided so that we're now at the lugubrious climax of the insipid 'It Must Be June'. Ann and Lorraine are still wisecracking their way through. As the number wends its way towards a sluggish conclusion, Lorraine is hoisted up in a kind of garden-swing formation and goosed twice, on the beat. ('You have the busiest hands,' she snaps at the pokerfaced chorus boy.) Marsh is simply gazing up at the heavens. Finally, just as Lawler and Brock appear under the bower, he stops the number with a shout, 'That'll be about enough of that – it smells.' 'Don't you like it?' asks lyricist Harry Warren, playing himself. In reply, Marsh harks back to the Ziegfeld stone age: 'I've liked it since 1905 – what do you think, we're putting on a revival?' (This archaic number is a backhand swipe at the failures of 1930; the insipid sentiment even has a Hooverian tinge. *42nd Street*, by contrast, epitomises the streamlined modernity of 1933, particularly once the edgy dialogue and showbiz excitement give way to the numbers.)

Outside the stage door of the 42nd Street Theater, Pat Denning (George Brent) is waiting for Dorothy Brock. She exits, giving him a discreet signal. He follows her into a cab and starts complaining that these clandestine meetings make him feel like a 'criminal'. She beams and kisses him enthusiastically, exclaiming, 'There's nothing criminal in that, is there?' For the first time in the movie, the pace slows down to allow for some dramatic intrigue. In the world of *42nd Street*, Denning is the personification of plot complications.

Brent's life, at least as it has been recounted, is somewhat more interesting than his persona. In his teens he appeared with the Abbey Players while serving as a courier for rebel leader Michael Collins, and supposedly fled Ireland with a price on his head. After appearing on the New York stage, he was picked by Ruth Chatterton – Warners' most prestigious female dramatic property – to co-star in *The Rich Are Always With Us* (1931). He subsequently married Chatterton after they appeared together in *The Crash* (1932). Touted as 'another Gable' and ranked by *Screen Book* with Jean Harlow as one of the comers of 1932, Brent proved the most reliable of Warners romantic leads, making forty-five movies from 1932–42, with six others besides *42nd Street* (which clearly plays on his gigolo potential) released in 1933 alone.

The back-seat romance dissolves to Marsh, in smoking jacket, fiddling with a model of the set as Jones and Barry explain that Brock is two-timing Dillon – and his $70,000 investment – with Denning, her old flame. (Ned Sparks typically makes the most of the scene, droning on about leaving his wife in a restaurant holding the bill, referring to Dillon as a 'Bulgarian boll weevil mourning its firstborn'.) Marsh, who is still smoking and drinking, wastes no time in taking decisive action. Muttering that 'no vaudeville chump is going to ruin my show', he telephones gangster Slim Murphy. Jones and Barry are terrified but Marsh not only knows exactly which pool hall to phone, he handles Murphy as though he's been commanding muscle all his life: 'Listen to me and get this …'

Murphy, who has to have the name Denning spelled out for him, is pleased to act as Marsh's enforcer, asking only to be remembered with 'ducats for the new show'. Meanwhile, Denning and Brock are finishing dinner at an unpretentious restaurant with a red-checked tablecloth and her theme, 'You're Getting to be a Habit with Me', swirling in the background. Denning won't let the fur-swathed Brock pick up the bill. 'There's a name for men who take money.' He then assures her that she's got ahead in her career because she 'deserved it' while he's stayed behind in vaudeville because that's where he belongs.

At the next morning's rehearsal, you can practically smell the flop sweat. The frantic sound of tapping is all but drowned out by Marsh's own stamping. 'Faster, faster, faster,' he screams, and then, 'Stop it, stop it – it's brutal.' Voice breaking, Marsh cites *Pretty Lady*'s imminent out-of-town opening, then pleads with the cast to show him something. Desperate tap gyrations resume. By now even the lecherous Dillon is

George Brent and Bebe Daniels at dinner

bored with the dancing, although he immediately wakes up when Dorothy Brock hops up on the piano to sing her number.

Rehearsals grind on, there's a superimposition of the clock spinning. Slave-driver Marsh is shrieking for the chorus to pick up the pace until poor Sawyer just collapses in a slow faint. As they drag her out, Marsh shouts for them to continue: 'This is a rehearsal, not a rest cure.' The solicitous Billy Lawler brings Sawyer a glass of water. (If you look fast, you can see Henry Walthall standing watching.) Somehow, Sawyer winds up next to Pat Denning who, nothing but time on his hands, turns flirtatious. 'Let's sit this one out,' he suggests. 'And if I lose my job?' she counters, raising again the economic imperative. 'Then there just won't be any show,' he answers in a joke that implies foreknowledge of the entire film.

More startling than this bit of precognitive humour is that a real chemistry seems to be happening. Suddenly, the supposedly love-smitten Denning and the allegedly innocent Sawyer are swapping innuendos about him pouring his ideas into her waiting ears. As the company is dismissed, Sawyer takes coquettish leave: 'Thanks doctor, your prescription was great.' After Dillon emerges with Brock, a

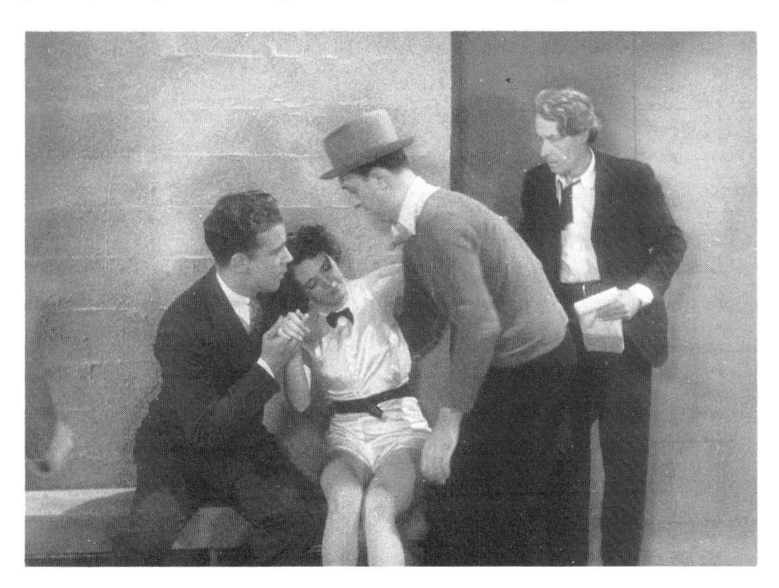

'Poor Sawyer just collapses': Dick Powell, Ruby Keeler, Allen Jenkins, Henry B. Walthall

smirking Denning trails them until Brock signals him to get lost. On the effortless rebound, he picks up Sawyer for dinner. Denning walks Sawyer back to her boarding-house, a desultory set with no resemblance to a New York street, but after they say goodnight he is attacked by Slim Murphy and his cohorts. The distraught Sawyer brings him upstairs to her room, where they're discovered by a comically disapproving Irish landlady who lectures the innocent couple on their impropriety while, behind her ample back, a lounge lizard in suspenders ostentatiously tiptoes out of his girlfriend's room. Thus evicted for entertaining a male guest, Sawyer must choose between spending the night on a park bench or at Denning's place. She bravely opts for the latter, a choice bizarrely underscored by a dollop of sentimental music.

It is obviously her first time alone in a man's apartment. She fiddles with her collar and practically jumps in the air when, suavely dimming the lights, the master of the house offers her a shot of illegal booze: 'Just a couple of rose-coloured glasses – let's try them on and see how the world looks.' One sip, and she's nodding out on the couch, at once inflaming and thwarting Denning's desire. The sentimental music continues as he suddenly scoops her up, caveman-style – 'Pat, what are you doing? Please, Pat, put me down' – and carries her into the boudoir, dropping her on the bed. In one of her most graceful movements, Keeler hits the mattress and, as if on a trampoline, bounds up into a sitting position in one smooth arc.

Sawyer's eyes couldn't possibly open any wider, but Denning just chuckles reassuringly. He tells the 'youngster' to get some sleep, not to worry, he'll use the couch. She's comforted but has evidently learned something about life on 42nd Street. After Denning leaves, she quickly shuts the door and – as the camera dollies in – locks it. Next morning there's still more tapping, at one point all imagination failing as the chorus simply jumps up and down in time. The rehearsal is so protracted that Jerry the pianist falls asleep on his stool. Evidently, in Sawyer's absence, they've been going all night, because when Brock drops in to see Denning she immediately notices that he's had a guest ('Oh, tea for two').

Brock also discovers that Denning is leaving New York for a stock job (a job!) in Philadelphia. They have another heart-to-heart, her signature song playing in the background. The scene drags on, with the amiable George Brent's total lack of conviction only heightened by Bebe Daniels's eye-blinking intensity. At last Brock thinks she's got it figured out. 'My success has been your failure,' she tells Denning, urging him to venture out on his own. *42nd Street* is unrelenting in its insistence on the importance of finding gainful employment, producing economic opportunity, generating cash. It never stops demanding selfless teamwork and strong leadership. It is obsessed with the representation of 'work'. By now, the rehearsal can only be represented as a kaleidoscope of female faces and rotating limbs. But the boss still isn't satisfied. Marsh is screaming like a madman, so agitated in his sarcasm that his voice breaks: 'What is this, amateur night? I am in the right theatre, am I not?' He reminds the cast that *Pretty Lady* is scheduled to open in Philadelphia the next evening.

While Philadelphia's reputation for sobriety occasions jokes among the chorines, Brock is stricken. 'Julian, you mean Atlantic City, don't you?' she pleads. He assures her that he does not. Understanding that fate is steering her back to Denning, Brock panics: 'But I don't want to go to Philadelphia!' 'Who does?' Marsh agrees. 'We couldn't get the house in Atlantic City.' 'But why Philadelphia?' Brock asks the gods. 'Well,' replies Marsh dreamily, 'when you become stage director we'll open in your apartment if you say so – but right now, it's Philadelphia!'

Rehearsals have adjourned to the Arch Street Theatre, a real venue in the City of Brotherly Love. There's the requisite backstage clatter, close-ups of chorus girl legs, another little exchange between Sawyer and Lawler. And Miss Brock, elegant in long gloves and a shoulder-padded satin gown, finally performs her big number, 'You're Getting to be a Habit with Me'. The mildly daring lyrics compare love to drug addiction but it's a perky torch song for all that – with Bebe Daniels gamely putting it across, clapping a bit at one point as if to psyche herself up. She can't really dance, but she's flanked by two chorus boys who can push her weight around. Another two join the ensemble and, leaning against them, Daniels executes a kind of striding soft-shoe. The number is shot so that we can see the orchestra, and enlivened with a bit of backstage business (MacElroy, trying to score with a chorine, absurdly demonstrates how she should prance about during 'Young and Healthy'). It also concludes with a bizarre punch-

Above: Dick Powell and Ruby Keeler
Below: 'Close-ups of chorus girl legs'

line. After flirting with each of the four chorus boys, Brock spots her real lover, a grinning simulacrum of a loincloth-wearing Mahatma Gandhi who trucks onstage to escort her off. (One wonders if this odd bit of showbiz free association has anything to do with Gandhi's well-publicised hunger strike while *42nd Street* was in production.)

As the final rehearsal ends – the curtain descending, as seen from stage – a depressed Marsh addresses the cast. (Cut from the final version is the scene where Henry Walthall dies on stage.) Then everyone disperses. Billy Lawler invites Peggy Sawyer to dinner but he's too late – she already has a date to attend the chorus party at a hotel. Andy Lee is off with a giggling Lorraine (he's just told her an off-colour story), but her mood curdles when Lee gets shanghaied by the weary, distracted Marsh. Referring to himself as a 'sick man' and not a machine, Marsh tells Lee that for the first time he's counting on someone else. It's almost a proposition: 'Come home with me, I'm lonesome.'

Sawyer bumps into Pat Denning on the street and, never missing a beat, he tries to pick her up, hoping she'll come to a 'nice cosy midnight snack that you read about'. (Although she demurs, it's one of the movie's minor pleasures that Sawyer – or Keeler – really does light up for him.) Just then the pair are spotted by Dorothy Brock who, saddled with the amorous Abner Dillon, bitches in the cab en route to another party at the hotel. 'Don't being with me just cheer you up?' Dillon makes the mistake of asking. 'Oh, tremendously,' Brock replies, 'I'm practically hysterical right now.'

The party is held in Brock's suite and Dillon acts the fool, boasting about his strength, ripping a phonebook in half. He tries to catch a dame but misjudges her leap and dumps her on the floor. She gets up and slaps his face; he whacks her posterior. Meanwhile Brock, who has been drinking and is again squabbling with her nemesis the playwright, storms into her bedroom. To add to the confusion, a tipsy Anytime Annie butts in, blaming an attack of hiccoughs on her tight shoes.

When producer Jones asks the distraught Dillon if he's going to be a 'sucker' for Brock's tantrum, Dillon goes paranoid, ranting that they've all been calling him a 'sucker' behind his back. He laboriously snaps his fingers and warns that Brock 'better not try to give me the air'.

Brock returns in a cold fury, tells Dillon that that's exactly what she's doing – making her point by calling him a 'sucker', slapping his face, throwing him out, and chucking a few champagne glasses in his wake. Everyone flees. Then teary-eyed Brock manages to put a phonecall through to Denning and pleads with him to come over.

Elsewhere at the hotel, Marsh is hoisting a glass, perhaps only water, and popping some pills when Jones and Barry burst in with the drunken Dillon, who is babbling that Brock is out of the show. 'Say, what is this, a game?' Marsh snarls, 'You can't do it!' When Dillon declares that the loss of $70,000 is his funeral, Marsh cuts him off: 'Yes – and the funeral of 200 other people as well.' Then he turns on the charm, flattering the befuddled manufacturer with the notion that 'Back in New York, they're calling you the angel of Broadway.' Dillon is partially mollified but he demands that Brock apologise to him tonight – 'and that's final'.

The chorus, blissfully unaware that the show is in jeopardy, is partying on the tenth floor. Pawed by the persistent Terry, Sawyer runs wildly out into the corridor and down a few flights where she spots Denning and then the producers. Brock draws Denning into her room

 The Mahatma Gandhi lookalike

and the producers withdraw, figuring they'll just have to fix the vaudeville chump again. Wide-eyed Sawyer takes it upon herself to warn Denning and knocks firmly on the door. But before she can deliver her message, she must deal with the drunken Brock, who lurches about screaming, 'You can't leave him alone for five minutes, can you? You want him for yourself, but you're not going to get him!' Denning tries to restrain her as she attacks Sawyer. Brock collapses and lies writhing on the floor, dress practically falling off as she shrieks that Sawyer has deliberately pushed her. Then the pain in her ankle sobers her up. The house doctor arrives, followed by Marsh: 'A broken ankle, huh – too bad it wasn't her neck!'

Next morning, Marsh cancels the performance but holds the company. The producers are frantic. It's incredible, but there's no understudy. Dillon appears with Anytime Annie: 'Your new leading lady – I guess I saved the day this time, folks.' There's a hasty conference, with Dillon relegated to holding Ann's pet Pekinese. Inexplicably, Ann herself has a change of heart. The idea 'sounded swell at breakfast', now she realises she can't carry the show – but there's someone who can – Sawyer! Marsh, increasingly disgusted with this turn of events, sighs in contempt. Although the notion of Ginger Rogers bowing out in favour of Ruby Keeler always amazes the modern viewer, Ann's altruism finally brings Marsh around. Andy Lee is sent to find Sawyer. 'Who me?' she gasps. 'The lead?' Marsh's eyebrows shoot up in exasperation. 'All right, I'll give you a chance – because I've got to. I'll either have a live leading lady or a dead chorus girl.' Then he sends everyone out.

Marsh has five hours to remodel Sawyer. This is archetypal showbiz stuff, featuring in such subsequent parodies as the off-Broadway musical *Dames at Sea*, Ken Russell's version of *The Boyfriend*, and the second half – 'Baxter's Beauties of 1933' – of Stanley Donen's *Movie Movie*. Indeed, it was already being parodied even before *42nd Street*. A backstage melodrama named *The Boyfriend* (no connection with the Russell film or the Sandy Wilson musical it adapts), which opened on Broadway in June 1932, included a chorus girl who understudies the show's leading lady and gets her chance to play the role on opening night. 'Her failure to make good is one of the original bits of the play,' one New York critic noted.

As an indication of just how tough this is going to be, Marsh and Sawyer get hung up rehearsing her opening line: 'Jim, they didn't tell me you were here. It was grand of you to come.' Sawyer can't seem to give it the necessary feeling. 'Have you ever been in love? Have you ever had a man hold you in his arms and kiss you?' Marsh demands. Sawyer shakes her head. Marsh, evidently a primitive exponent of the Method, grabs her in an embrace so passionate you wonder if he's insinuated his tongue down her throat. In any case, it's enough to get her to gasp her way through the line.

Then on to the songs, with Jerry the pianist pounding away as Sawyer launches into 'Come and meet those dancing feet ...' before sobbing, 'I can't, I can't.' But Marsh won't let her quit. There's a wipe to her frantically hoofing before the curtain. 'That's fair, only fair,' Marsh mutters, betraying a trace of optimism. One hour to curtain. Marsh is fierce. 'You let me down, Sawyer,' he warns, but his threatening grab melts into a tender hug. He tells her that she's definitely going on. The word goes out to an excited cast.

Billy Lawler materialises with coffee and some sentimental background music. It's their scene. Sawyer thinks that maybe she's dreaming. Lawler claims he's been for her ever since the day she walked in on him in his BVDs: 'You know what I mean, don't you?' Even coyer than he, she shakes her head no. Finally, they kiss. 'The transfer is complete,' as Rick Altman notes; Lawler 'declares his love and returns sexual significance to kissing. By intertwining stage success with sexual initiation, this sequence sets the stage for the show to follow.' But there's one bit of unfinished Oedipal business. Enter the glaring Brock, who was after all playing opposite Lawler on the stage. Lawler makes a feeble attempt to kick her out but she orders him away, closing the door with a well-aimed crutch (a bit of business exuberantly reprised by the unbilled Glenda Jackson in Russell's *The Boyfriend*).

'So you're going to take my place?' Brock begins. Sawyer is petrified. 'You're nervous, aren't you?' the star demands accusingly, 'Well, don't be ...' Brock's theme wafts up again as she prepares to extend her benediction. 'When I started for the theatre tonight, I wanted to tear your hair out. And then I started thinking, well, I've had my chance.' Paying her replacement a neat backhanded compliment ('You know, Peggy, 'most anyone can have success with the proper breaks'),

Brock announces that she and Denning are going to marry – she'll take Pat and vaudeville 'or whatever comes with it'.

It's the moment of truth. The theatre marquee reads, 'Pretty Lady Gala Premiere'. The conductor taps his baton, the orchestra bursts into the overture as, backstage, the chorus scrambles downstairs (affording us another peek at their thighs under the frilly dresses). Brock is trembling as Sawyer gets dressed, delivering the penultimate line of camp absurdity: 'Now go out there and be so swell, you'll make me hate you!' The curtain rises and the chorus, dressed as Southern belles, kicks its way out before the audience. Backstage, Marsh is pacing. Once again, the economic imperative asserts itself. He pulls Sawyer aside for his speech: 'Two hundred people, 200 jobs, $200,000, five weeks of grind and blood and sweat depend on you. It's the lives of all these people ... you've got to give and give and give ...'

The camera closes in for 'the famous command', as Ethan Mordden called it, 'half shopgirl's dream and half egalitarian imperative'. Marsh grabs the compliantly ga-ga Sawyer, smiling up at him and nodding like a dummy: 'You're going out a youngster, but you've got to come back a star.' Marsh shoves Sawyer out on stage to cheers from the ensemble. 'Why, Jim, they didn't tell me you were here. It was grand of you to come ...' She still can't say the line but, at this point, who cares? The sudden shout, 'All aboard the Niagara Limited', announces that the train is in the station. Finally, some 73 minutes into the movie, the first of the Busby Berkeley numbers is about to burst the narrative asunder.

To underscore the apparent non sequitur, the nameless character whom Sawyer plays is poised to leave for her honeymoon – to 'Shuffle off to Buffalo' as the song title has it – and not, it would seem, with Jim, whom one supposes she might otherwise have expected to see. But there's no time to think. A smarmy-looking lounge lizard (the Ziegfeld veteran Clarence Nordstrom) has a 'Just Married' sign affixed to his back, by Jim no less, and begins serenading the delighted Sawyer, cheek to cheek: 'I'll go home and pack my panties, you go home and get your scanties and away we'll go ...'

With the song's second chorus the camera retreats as the caboose from which the couple sing abruptly splits into a cross-section of a train (another Ziegfeld touch – his 1921 *Follies* had an actual subway car

 'Shuffle Off to Buffalo'

JUST
MARRIED

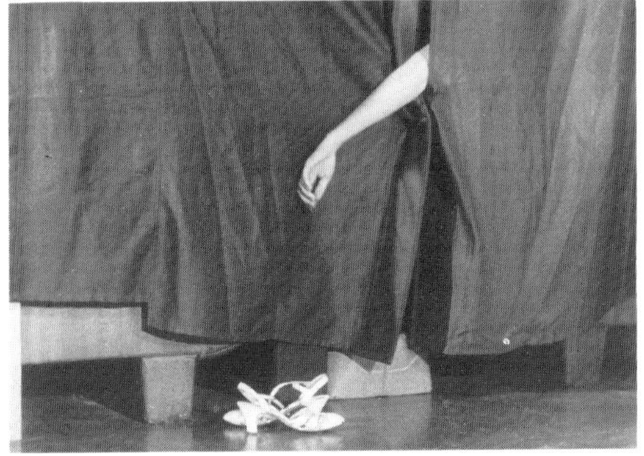

onstage). There's a musical interlude as the camera tracks back even further from the performers to include an applauding audience in the scene. Then the newlyweds skip-slide through the train as an assortment of passengers point and laugh. Wide-eyed Sawyer is about to lose her innocence, and the third chorus is picked up by the two sniggering 'bad girls' who have been her mentors.

Lorraine and Ann, both wearing silk negligées and perched in an upper berth brazenly eating the fruits of knowledge (an apple and a banana), giggle that 'Matrimony is baloney, she'll be wanting alimony in a year or so.' Oblivious to this cynical ridicule, Sawyer and her partner do a softshoe in their pyjamas, then sit coyly down on their berth as the Busby Berkeley chorine cornucopia spills its largess. The newlyweds' narrative is at once eclipsed and supported by a spectacle of erotic abundance. The song is now sung by the ensemble, grouped two-by-two in the sleeping compartments (one couple, of course, caught by surprise) in preparation for what promises to be a mass pyjama party cum crypto-lesbian honeymoon.

Night falls and the prancing Pullman porter struts down the empty corridor collecting shoes to shine. Sawyer, sequestered in a compartment with her new husband, extends an arm to deposit her own little pumps. An invisible act of passion within inspires a surprised squeal; her arm quickly rises and slowly falls as she limply drops her shoes to the floor. The symbolic defloration is rhymed after a fashion by a cut to the porter shining himself to sleep, his masturbatory motions gradually ceasing and his snore blending into the train whistle.

There's no rest for the weary, however. Backstage, Marsh is dragging on his cigarette and screaming at Sawyer to 'rest and relax'. It's time for the other young star to show his stuff. Bursting into 'I'm Young and Healthy', Dick Powell bounces on the balls of his feet and rocks forward to sing. (This odd list suggests a corset beneath his tuxedo, even as his vocalising has the timbre of a constricted saxophone.) The gesticulating Powell assumes a rapid succession of stiff poses, first outside the curtain and then against a black backdrop, as he serenades the cheerful platinum blonde who reclines, her shoulders invitingly bare, upon a garden bench. She is Toby Wing, a 17-year-old ex-Keystone Girl, and her mischievous, chevron-shaped smile is never for a moment dropped to allow the utterance of even a single word.

Overleaf: 'Glorifying the American girl'

Singing the praises of the 'snooty little cutie', who never pantomimes less than utter approval, Powell swarms around her as the bench melts into the stage.

While Powell cradles Wing on a revolving turntable, they are closely observed – and not only by us. Berkeley first cuts to an ostentatious high-angle shot, then returns to ground level to surround the couple with a formation of chorus boys flat on their stomachs, as if crawling out of the trenches, who nod their heads and groan in sympathy. All rise and dance around Wing, escorting her onto an invisible treadmill where she leads a succession of veiled chorus girls (including a mildly forward Ginger Rogers) past Powell, who by this time is bellowing his way into the fourth chorus: 'Ohhh! I'm young and healthy ...' Summoned by this ardour, Wing steps off the moving stage into Powell's arms and they kiss in close-up.

Berkeley is now in his element, surrounding the couple with a geometric formation of scantily dressed chorines, their legs akimbo on the rotating reflective surface. Ziegfeld's means of 'glorifying the American girl' had the dynamic chorus intermittently reform itself as a

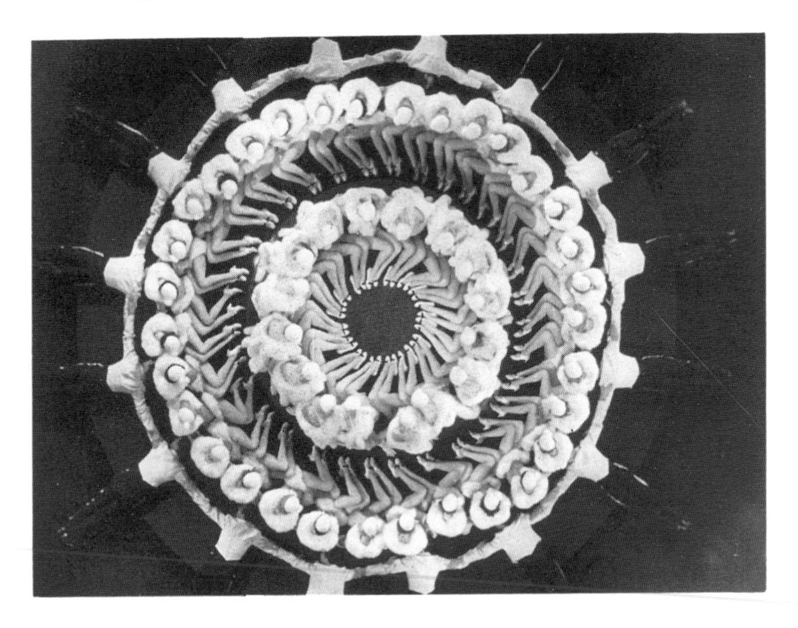

'Geometric formation of scantily dressed chorines'

seductively pulsating floral vortex. Berkeley perfects this strategy by using the close-up briefly to individualise the identically dressed, synthesised chorines, and the crane shot to accentuate the abstract patterns to which they submit – in each case demonstrating the dreamlike superiority of the movies, which is to say the illusion of mastery which the cinema substitutes for actual presence.

In her essay 'The Image of Woman as Image: The Optical Politics of *Dames*', Lucy Fischer writes that 'the cinematic image of woman' as male projection and object of desire is hyperbolised by the zombie-like trance and dissociated smiles of the Berkeley girls, performances which 'extend passivity into catatonia'. Here, perfectly blonde and endlessly reproduced, is the robot love-goddess of *Metropolis*. No wonder Zanuck was impressed with the number. The sequence is the Dream Factory's dream. Fantasy is rationalised, depression dispelled with interchangeable sex dolls manufactured in delirious profusion before (and for) the spectator's eye.

While 'Shuffle off to Buffalo' evokes an eroticised technology by staging a wedding night on a speeding express train, 'I'm Young and Healthy' embodies the relationship between libido and mechanical apparatus. The industrial quality of the experience is heightened in that the soundtrack activates the image. 'I'm Young and Healthy' exemplifies the 'double paradigm' that Rick Altman finds characteristic of Berkeley production numbers, the binary oppositions of the female image/male voice and the male spectator/female auditor: 'By identifying woman with dancing and man with song, woman with the image track and man with the sound track, the backstage musical of the thirties thus puts the particularities of its technological heritage to work thematically.'

The desiring machine grinds on. A succession of parted chorus girl thighs pass by the camera. Then, the female chorus chased by its male counterpart, the dancers engage in a bit of trucking as small lines of four form during the musical break. The women advance towards the viewer with mounting excitement – their Maxfactorised bodies fragmented into gigantic close-ups of perfectly swaying knees and hands inserted, without thinking, in white fur muffs. Although an overhead view is followed by a brief shot from the audience, such inscription is rare. In general, Berkeley smashes the proscenium (and indeed all visual logic) to allow the pure pleasure of unmediated looking.

Women multiply and objects mutate. Berkeley's blatantly spectacular fantasies suggest, in their visionary excess, the Baudelairean description of a man in a crowd as 'a kaleidoscope equipped with consciousness', except that this is a kaleidoscope of unconsciousness. Personal responsibility dissolves in an orgy of plenitude. Picking up ribbons to create another geometric formation, the chorus girls are offered up as if on a wedding cake. There's an overhead 'camera iris'. The climactic camera motion penetrates a corridor of chorine legs for a close-up of the smiling Wing and Powell, completing the identification between the spectator's gaze and Berkeley's motorised phallus.

Such direct address, in which an event is offered to the spectator by a cinema showman, defines what Tom Gunning has theorised, after Eisenstein, as the Cinema of Attractions. (Even the more sober, social-minded viewer must note: So many people working on the screen!) What had previously been backstage voyeurism has just been placed front and centre. In the movie's 'backstage', we see Anytime Annie – already in costume for the next number – expressing her pleasure that Peggy Sawyer is a hit. Abner Dillon, though, has been dozing through the entire show, apparently indifferent to his investment. A surrealist reading of *42nd Street* would suggest that the last number is the kiddie-car manufacturer's dream. In waking life, however, he has forgotten his duty to walk Ann's dog which, with her hysterical prompting, he abjectly does.

Thus the putative Angel of Broadway may not even be present for the grand finale and title-song. A somewhat more confident Ruby Keeler appears centre stage in a white derby and grown-up slit skirt (but still with puffy shoulders) as the curtain parts on a New York City street scene. Having supplanted Bebe Daniels's Brock as the personification of the metropolis, Keeler sways suggestively as she sings about 'that little thoroughfare' in 'the heart of old New York', a magnet for women from all over the city. (Whatever one makes of Keeler's practised innocence, there's no missing the pure New Yorkese with which she describes the succession of girls who, side by side, are 'glawri-fiiied'.)

Keeler invites us to 'come and meet those dancing feet'. At the musical break, she strips off and tosses away her skirt to embark upon a remarkably determined tap routine. Thudding away, doggedly on the beat, she no more misses a step than she takes her eyes off her feet. The first of several 'invisible' match-cuts used in the sequence transforms her stage into the roof of a taxicab stuck in 42nd Street traffic. Keeler taps a bit more, climbs down, then hops up on the running-board. The cab whisks her away to reveal a frantic street scene cum freak show – a mad commotion in which everyone in the choreographed crowd is moving to the same brassy beat.

The vision suggests a Max Fleischer cartoon or a syncopated UFA nightmare. It's as if humanity itself has become anthropomorphised: there's a huge dancing cop, a shuffling sandwich man, patrons strutting in and out of a barber shop. An apple vendor juggles his wares, a nurse slaps her baby's bottom as if it were a stand-up bass, an enormous black doorman blows his whistle, a pair of fruit vendors take off to play golf. Street urchins tap, a cigar-store Indian comes to life; with the close-up of a tabloid extra, a lurid narrative begins to coalesce. There's a scream as a wild-eyed man bursts into a hotel room and shoots out the light. The camera pans up and into the window, then retreats as a young woman clambers out and, avidly watched by a crowd at street level, swan dives down into a man's arms. Demonstrating no little aplomb, she immediately starts dancing until stabbed in the back by the jealous man who had invaded her room.

A musical sex-murder for our entertainment. Blearily hoisting an illegal intoxicant as the sound of police sirens is heard, *bon vivant* Dick Powell gazes out from the window of a second-floor speakeasy (the bartender mixing more cocktails in the background) to pick up the verse with the jaded observation that 'the big parade goes on for years'. Once Powell invokes the sacred name '42nd Street', however, the camera pans across to a chorus, positioned in the 42nd Street set. Although the New Amsterdam theatre that housed Ziegfeld's *Follies* is visible in the foreground, this is clearly the more democratic and degraded street of 1933.

Identically dressed in Keeler's original costume, puffy shoulders and all, the chorines execute a saucy sideways swish before being joined by the chorus boys, who lift them up to kick their legs. As the chorus turn their backs and mount the stairs that have unobtrusively appeared, placards affixed to their backs form an animated image of the New York skyline. The most conventional of the three production numbers, this homage to New York has many precursors. The 1929 talkie *Broadway* featured a deco nightclub full of chorines in skyscraper headgear; the highlight of the Twelfth Beaux Arts Ball, held in January 1931, was a 'Fantasy in Flame and Silver' in which a number of prominent Manhattan architects appeared costumed as 'The Skyline of New York'. That same year, the climax of the last *Ziegfeld Follies* was 'Doing the New York', with the entire company cavorting in front of a set representing the new Empire State Building.

The buildings sway, the lyrics are reprised: 'Hear the beat of dancing feet ...' There's a match-cut so that the chorus can exit off a stairway that resembles a prone Empire State. A fool for love, King Kong had all but simultaneously fallen from that monumental edifice; here, the building itself lies prostrate. In a wobbly movement that echoes the desultory aerial shot of the opening montage, the camera dollies up to frame Keeler and Powell at the top, waving to the audience from the apex of success.

In contrast to the more democratic distribution of close-ups in the previous numbers, the camera here anoints Keeler as star. If, as has been suggested, the tension that underlies the musical form is that between the romantic imagination embodied in the musical numbers and the narrative restraints of the 'realistic' social order, then the work of staging a successful Broadway show, the reward of achieving stardom, and the miracle of bringing together a viable pair of romantic lovers are brought to fruition and celebrated in this utopian finale. Having conquered New York, as the cinema – thanks to Busby Berkeley – has most definitely conquered the stage, Keeler and Powell coyly conceal their embrace, drawing down from heaven an asbestos curtain. This anti-Promethean gesture at once serves to naturalise the impossible spectacle just witnessed and effectively to rationalise the orgiastic plenitude of the previous fifteen minutes into a single, chaste and unseen kiss.

For the movie's reviewers and audiences, *42nd Street* more than lived up to its publicity, even though most commentators deemed the premise overfamiliar. *42nd Street*, wrote the *New York Times*, was 'the liveliest and one of the most tuneful screen musical comedies that has come out of Hollywood.' The *New York Herald Tribune* found it 'brisk and alert', particularly in comparison to the previous glut of backstage movies. Hearst's *New York American* thought *42nd Street* brought 'musicals back with a great big bang', reporting that the opening night crowd applauded the dance numbers. The *New York World-Telegram* felt the movie 'too lavish, perhaps' but the *Daily News* correctly predicted 'a box-office smash'. In any case, the New Deal in Entertainment had arrived. Echoing the radio-broadcast 'fireside chat' which the new President delivered on 12 March, Warners took an ad in *Variety* to announce that 'America's Pocketbook is Open for Business. No Shutdown – No Letdown – but a SHOWDOWN in the war against depression. Whether you're a Democrat or a Republican you'll endorse – WARNER BROS' 10-WEEK RECONSTRUCTION PROGRAM.'

The week that *42nd Street* opened in New York, the Hollywood studios, led by MGM, initiated a temporary 50 per cent pay cut for all salaried employees. Zanuck, who had his own salary slashed, opposed the reductions and attempted to rescind them. Not only was he overruled, but Harry Warner threatened to extend the cuts beyond the initial eight-week period. 'Furious and shaken,' historian Thomas Schatz writes, Zanuck 'conducted studio business with an air of detachment and was all but oblivious to the tremendous impact of *42nd Street*.' On 15 April, he resigned.

Hence the appropriateness of the morose *42nd Street* coda: a crowd in evening clothes leaves the theatre, bizarrely complaining that Julian Marsh is taking unjustified credit for the discovery of that new sensation, Peggy Sawyer. Marsh stands off to the side unrecognised, listening ironically and holding his stomach, the ubiquitous cigarette dangling from his lips. As the show-within-the-show ended with Sawyer and her consort on top of the world, the 'real' show concludes with the lonely stage-director sitting on the bottom rung of a fire-escape in a dark alley.

Before the fade-out there are a few wistful bars of Brock's theme, as if to suggest that the former silent stars, Baxter and Daniels, are being supplanted by the 'Young and Healthy' Keeler and Powell. It's a distinctly downbeat close – but then the whole finale is a kind of fantastic wish fulfilment. Peggy Sawyer may have flattened the Empire State, but the show itself is still in Philadelphia.

Overleaf: 'the lonely stage director . . . in a dark alley'

IV

Still in the swaddling clothes of the talkie stage in 1933, Hollywood felt a desperate need for romantic leading men who could both mug and talk expertly. By September of that year it had signed 315 actors from legit. … The prevailing trend on the lots that year was the filmusical, in an attempt to jump on the bandwagon of Warner Bros' *42nd Street.* … Top movie personality of 1933, however, was conceded to be Franklin D. Roosevelt in the newsreels, termed by a Hollywood wit, 'the Barrymore of the White House'.

Abel Green and Joe Laurie Jr., *Show Biz: From Vaude to Video* (1951)

On 2 May 1933, *42nd Street* completed its run at the Strand. *Variety* reported that the movie had grossed nearly $170,000 in less than seven weeks, 'some kind of record these days'. (Box-office receipts bottomed out that spring at 40 per cent of the figure in January 1931, when *Little Caesar* took in $190,000 in four weeks at the Strand.) Indeed *Variety*,

Ruby Keeler with director Lloyd Bacon

which a few weeks later cited *42nd Street* prominently among those recent releases 'that clicked in most small towns', observed that the movie 'would have stayed an additional week or two [at the Strand] but for complaint from Loew's that it should get the picture'.

42nd Street was the top box-office attraction for the first half of 1933, according to the *Motion Picture Herald*, and Warners was already prepared with a replacement. *Gold Diggers of 1933* had its world premiere at two Denver theatres on 30 May; on 6 June, it began a ten-week run at Grauman's Chinese in Hollywood and two days later opened at the Strand. 'Let me tell you about my Operation,' Cincinnati exhibitor Ike Libson was quoted in a full-page *Variety* ad.

> Warner Bros. are to be congratulated for providing leadership at a time when the industry needed a leader. Especially commendable is their action in making *Gold Diggers of 1933* immediately available. Two pictures like *42nd Street* and *Gold Diggers* within a few weeks of each other are the finest business stimulants possible. ... I am signing a 1933–34 Warner contract now because I have confidence in America, the Industry and Warner Bros.

Footlight Parade, which went into production in June and was released in October 1933, reunited most of the *42nd Street* principals: directors Lloyd Bacon and Busby Berkeley (who was simultaneously staging the dances for his last Goldwyn-produced Cantor vehicle, *Roman Scandals*), songwriters Warren and Dubin, screenwriter James Seymour, stars Ruby Keeler and Dick Powell, supporting players Guy Kibbee and Allen Jenkins. Joan Blondell was added from *Gold Diggers of 1933* and James Cagney, Warners' number one male star, took the role similar to Warner Baxter's Julian Marsh.

At the end of the year, with the crisis averted (at least for the movie industry), the *Motion Picture Herald* ranked *Gold Diggers* second and *42nd Street* third in its list of 1933's top money-makers, just behind the year's greatest attraction, Mae West in *I'm No Angel*, which opened in October and somewhat eclipsed *Footlight Parade*. *42nd Street* was ranked second in *Film Daily*'s annual ten best list and was nominated for two Academy awards, best picture and best sound recording.

42nd Street is inextricably bound up in the experience of the

Depression and the coming of the New Deal. Its production spans the 1932 Presidential election campaign and its release – together with that of *Gold Diggers of 1933*, which opened in Los Angeles and New York the very week that Congress passed the National Recovery Act – coincided almost exactly with the celebrated 'first hundred days' of the Roosevelt administration. (The only other film so spectacularly to embody the popular mood was Disney's animated short *The Three Little Pigs* which, released a few days before *Gold Diggers*, provided an even catchier anti-Depression anthem than 'We're in the Money', with 'Who's Afraid of the Big Bad Wolf?') Thus *42nd Street* is one of a handful of Hollywood movies which not only reflect but *are* American social history – films that might include *Casablanca*, the original *Invasion of the Body Snatchers*, *Bonnie and Clyde*, *Rocky* and *Ghostbusters*.

On the one hand, *42nd Street* is a Horatio Alger story as refracted through the Ziegfeld *Follies*: the virtuous Peggy Sawyer works hard, resists temptation, gets her break, and makes the most of it. On the other hand, the film offers the vision of some new, collective social order, founded on the industrial production of erotic fantasy, the joyous orchestration of the masses, the confusion between making love and making work. Even more than most musicals, *42nd Street* presents 'head-on', as Richard Dyer suggests in his essay on the use-value of entertainment, just 'what utopia would feel like'.

One can no more miss the connection between the show/movie/number's forceful director(s) and the political vacuum concurrently perceived in American life, than deny that the myth of individual initiative is viscerally subsumed by the logic of the dance sequences and indeed the entire show: talent is ultimately less important in *42nd Street* than cooperation. (Hence perhaps the inspirational spectacle of mediocrities like the Ruby Keeler and Dick Powell characters elevated to stardom.) And cooperation is a function of direction. Dorothy Brock, the temperamental star, is a replaceable cog in a vast machine, while the success of Peggy Sawyer is at once predicated on an ability to follow orders and dependent on the cooperation of 200 individuals under the rule of a single, despotic leader.

As Mark Roth points out in 'Some Warners Musicals and the Spirit of the New Deal', this change in the American ethos is precisely that put forth by Roosevelt in his Inaugural address.

> If I have read the temper of our people correctly, we now realize as we have never realized before our interdependence. … If we are to go forward, we must move as a trained and loyal army willing to sacrifice for the good of a common discipline.

(It was this reference to martial 'unity' which, much to the dismay of the new President's wife Eleanor, occasioned the greatest ovation from the crowd.)

> In their need [the people of the United States] have registered a mandate that they want direct, vigorous action. They have asked for discipline and direction under leadership. They have made me the present instrument of their wishes.

As for the past instrument of their wishes, Julian Marsh is last seen sitting weary and alone. His final words (the last in the film) are cynical and resigned: 'Just another show.' The business cycle is the unchanging wheel of *dharma*. If, as Roth suggests, Baxter is a pre-New Deal man, forceful but less confident than his successor James Cagney, *42nd Street* is also a pre-New Deal world, more desperate and sordid than that of *Footlight Parade* (which climaxes with a full military tribute to Roosevelt and the NRA). Nevertheless, the *Los Angeles Times* reported that '*42nd Street* has seemingly made Warner Baxter a hero of the hour.'

Of course, Baxter's Marsh was only one of many potential Roosevelts offered to the American public during the winter of 1932–3. Even before the US publication of *Gabriel Over the White House*, Walter Wanger (who produced *American Madness* and *Washington Merry-Go-Round* at Columbia) had purchased the rights as the basis for his first picture at MGM. Realising that the messianic Jud Hammond could not help but suggest the President-elect, Wanger bypassed Hoover supporter Louis B. Mayer and took the project to Roosevelt partisan William Randolph Hearst, whose Cosmopolitan studio was then affiliated with MGM. Once Hearst had personally revised the script, the film was made quickly and cheaply with the aim of a wide national release on Inauguration Day.

When *Gabriel Over the White House* previewed on 1 March 1933, the *Hollywood Reporter* predicted that it could 'go down in the history of motion pictures as the most sensational piece of film entertainment the world has ever known'. *Variety* was no less impressed: 'At no time in the past 25 years was the US as ready and ripe for a production of this type as right now.' But Mayer, who had not previously seen the movie, was furious. Shipping the print to New York to be studied by the Hays Office and MGM president Nicholas Schenk, he managed to delay the premiere for almost a month by ordering numerous minor retakes.

Gabriel Over the White House appears to be *42nd Street*'s missing subtext. Heavily promoted as 'The ReBirth of a Nation', it showed Jud Hammond's transformation from an infantile, backslapping party politician to a patriarchal, ascetic dictator. As embodied by Walter Huston ('re-elected', so was said, to the screen presidency he held in *Abraham Lincoln*), his 'show' is blatantly programmatic. A vehicle for divine will, Hammond suspends Congress, declares martial law, conscripts the unemployed, 'muscles in on' (and summarily executes) the nation's gangsters, and strong-arms the European powers into paying their war debts, thus ending the Depression with a millennial Pax Americana.

As amplified by Hearst editorials, *Gabriel Over the White House* was at once a political manifesto and part of a debate on fascism that would continue throughout Roosevelt's first term. Yet unlike the fascist masterpiece *Triumph of the Will*, *Gabriel* makes little appeal to the collective libido – for that Hearst would have had to hire Berkeley to choreograph a goose-stepping chorus line of the unemployed. (Indeed, there is a bit of this in the mass 'Sieg-heil' tap dance Berkeley devised for the 'Lullaby of Broadway' number in *Gold Diggers of 1935*.)

The synthesis of *42nd Street* and *Gabriel Over the White House* arrived in April 1934 when, despite his eclipse by James Cagney in *Footlight Parade*, Warner Baxter took one more shot at screen leadership on his return to Fox. In *Stand Up and Cheer*, a 1934 release based on an idea by Will Rogers, Baxter plays Lawrence Cromwell, 'the world's recognised authority on feminine beauty and charm', who (despite his name) is drafted by the President of the United States to head the new Department of Amusement, a cross between Hollywood and the National Recovery Administration. 'The gist of this preposterous NRA propaganda musical,' explained David Platt in the left-wing journal *New Theatre*, 'is that the depression is a purely mental state. ... Mass campaigns of musical enlightenment are forthwith organized against poverty and misery.' At the climax of the show, the end of the

Depression is simply proclaimed. 'An insatiable longing for tap-dancing and mammy songs is created in the army of unemployed and hungry workers,' Platt noted, which is one way to describe the movie's utopian premise.

As *Stand Up and Cheer* launched Shirley Temple, the most significant Hollywood star of the mid-1930s, the one-two punch of *42nd Street* and *Gold Diggers of 1933* served to ignite several careers – including the teams of Keeler and Powell (who made another four films together) and Dubin and Warren (signed to a seven-year Warners contract). Even the mute Toby Wing was elevated to a minor celebrity. But although *Newsweek*'s review of *42nd Street* – which declared Keeler 'a more valuable piece of motion picture property than her more famous husband' – thought that Busby Berkeley had 'gone to a lot of ineffectual bother about his intricate formations', it was Berkeley's reputation that soared. The August 1934 issue of *Movie Classic* reported that after Keeler and Powell, Berkeley, who likewise received a seven-year contract, was the number three recipient of fan mail at Warner Bros.

Berkeley directed dance numbers for *Dames*, *Fashions of 1934*, and *Wonder Bar* (all 1934), before directing *Gold Diggers of 1935* in its entirety. For the remainder of the decade, he worked on increasingly formulaic musicals at the rate of four per year, despite heavy drinking and the distraction of three trials for manslaughter arising from a fatal car accident in September 1935. Berkeley left Warners (along with his colleagues Harry Dubin, Al Warren, Ruby Keeler and Dick Powell) when his contract expired in 1939. He made four Mickey Rooney and Judy Garland musicals at MGM, and supervised the dances for the 1941 *Ziegfeld Girl*.

After directing Carmen Miranda in *The Gang's All Here* (1943) while on loan to Fox, Berkeley found himself back at Warners as part of a deal designed to ship Joan Crawford out of MGM. Dumped and debt-ridden after a single abortive project, Berkeley returned to Broadway without success and, having attempted suicide during the summer of 1946, was committed to the psychopathic ward in Los Angeles General Hospital. He enjoyed a modest comeback at MGM with *Take Me Out to the Ball Game* (1949) and was able to prolong his Hollywood career for another five years. A string of unrealised film and TV projects was interrupted by some second-unit work on the 1962 Doris Day musical, *Jumbo*.

Berkeley was in 'semi-retirement' by the following year when the Spring 1963 *Film Culture* used a still from the notorious slave-market number in *Roman Scandals* as the cover illustration for an issue entirely devoted to Andrew Sarris's evaluation of American directors. Sarris placed Berkeley in the category of 'Likeable But Elusive', noting that 'if some of his socialized floral patterns do indeed look a bit naive and prematurely anti-Astairish today, they did have their time and place in the depths of the Depression when the difference between quality and quantity did not seem too important.' The slave-market cover was rhymed in *Film Culture*'s follow-up issue, devoted to the directors of the 'New American Cinema', with a production still from Jack Smith's *Normal Love* featuring an assortment of 'chorus cuties' on a giant wedding cake. Berkeley's significance for underground aesthetes may be gleaned by Smith's inclusion of 'all Busby Berkeley flix' in the list of 'secret flix' he invokes in the manifesto. 'The Perfect Filmic Appositeness of Maria Montez', published in the Winter 1962–3 issue of *Film Culture*; Susan Sontag's celebrated 'Notes on Camp', which first appeared in the Fall 1964, special Goldwater issue of *Partisan Review*, singles out Berkeley's numbers for *42nd Street* and *Gold Diggers of 1933* as 'pure' (because unintentional) camp.

The opening salvo in the Berkeley revival came in June 1965, when his 1942 MGM musical *For Me and My Gal* was shown as a special retrospective at the San Francisco Film Festival; in November, the Gallery of Modern Art in New York organised 'A Tribute to Busby Berkeley: Master Builder of the American Film', with Ruby Keeler in attendance. The series, which opened with *42nd Street*, received national coverage: 'They call me the King of Camp,' Berkeley told *Newsweek*. 'I didn't know what camp was, but Raymond Rohauer, who organized the show, explained to me that camp is anyone who reaches the top and does something unusual and enjoyable.'

The Berkeley tribute subsequently toured London, Munich, Vienna and Paris. The January 1966 issue of *Cahiers du Cinéma* featured an interview with Berkeley, while Jean-Louis Comolli's introduction proposed him as a primitive surrealist, comparing 'the American cineaste, explorer of dreams and of cinematographic language – or, rather, of the language of cinematographic dreams' to the eccentric modernist Raymond Roussel: 'Like the art of Roussel, that of Berkeley plays at the same time on the tableau of logic and on that of nonsense, plays on the coexistence of coherence and surprise.' (In similar vein, the March 1966 issue of *Positif* featured Robert Benayoun's appreciation, 'Berkeley le Centupleur'.)

In 1966, a 45-minute pastiche of *42nd Street* called *Dames at Sea or Golddiggers Afloat* opened in New York at the off-off-Broadway Cafe Cino, with Bernadette Peters in the role of Ruby, an aspiring actress who gets off the bus from Utah and, in a single day, becomes 'the toast of New York, a star of Broadway and the sweetheart of the Navy'. That fall, Berkeley began touring American colleges with a programme of clips called 'An Evening with Busby Berkeley and the Fabulous Era of Hollywood Musicals'. The show, according to a report published in the February 1967 issue of the *Film Society Review*, lasted nearly three hours and climaxed with the number '42nd Street'. The writer John Thomas, while attributing Berkeley's new popularity to camp, saw a deeper significance:

> It's no coincidence that the floral patterns created by the Berkeley Girls are all variations of the mandala, that circular, centered structure which C.G. Jung tells us is the basic integrating image within the human psyche. For Berkeley's numbers are not so much products of a mechanized age as of an age so disorganized that mechanization could be seen as a desirable goal.

A direct quotation from *Gold Diggers of 1933* appeared in 1967's *Bonnie and Clyde*, while in 1968 and 1969 a television variety show called 'Dean Martin Presents the Golddiggers' served as a summer replacement for 'The Dean Martin Show'. December 1968 saw an expanded *Dames at Sea* successfully restaged off-Broadway.

By March 1969, the revival was official; the *New York Times Sunday Magazine* ran a cover story entitled 'The golden age of Camp – A Busby Berkeley movie'. The article attributed Berkeley's comeback to television: 'Tonite! On the late, late, great, great show – a genuine, 1930's, film musical spectacular directed by Busby Berkeley. Groovy!' By this time, Sarris had expanded his *Film Culture* item on Berkeley for his book *The American Cinema: Directors and Directions 1929–1968*, noting that 'taken as a whole, Berkeley's contributions deserved better than being consigned to the sniggerings of Camp followers. Busby Berkeley deserves enduring respect as the Méliès of the Musical.'

In June 1969, Berkeley and Keeler made a surprise appearance at a Warner Bros junket with an 11-minute compilation film, *Busby Berkeley and the Gold Diggers*, shown later that summer as a short subject with Robert Downey's underground comedy *Putney Swope*. Soon after, producer Harry Rigby began plotting Berkeley's Broadway comeback, and announced a $500,000 Broadway revival of the 1925 Vincent Youmans musical comedy *No! No! Nanette*, to be directed by Berkeley and star Keeler. *Newsweek* reported that Rigby would be 'advertising the show in the underground papers because, as he told Berkeley, "You make head movies. The kids love to go to your films and get high on marijuana."'

When *No! No! Nanette* opened at the 46th Street Theatre on 19 January 1971, *Time* used its review to criticise the whole notion of camp, while other critics revealed that the 'long-stemmed line of Busby Berkeley Girls' were actually choreographed by Donald Saddler. On a more positive note, the 'Warner Bros. 1930s' issue of *The Velvet Light Trap* in spring 1971 included Mark Roth's influential essay, 'Some Warners Musicals and the Spirit of the New Deal', which declared that 'Roosevelt was a kind of political Busby Berkeley. ... The "little man" could trust Roosevelt as the individual chorus girl could trust Berkeley to see that their effort was not wasted, to see that each had his part to play.' The same year also saw a highly successful revival of Berkeley's Carmen Miranda vehicle *The Gang's All Here*, as well as the American opening of Ken Russell's *The Boyfriend*.

In 1973, Berkeley was the subject of two extensive bio-filmographies, *The Busby Berkeley Book* (lavishly published by the New York Graphic Society), and *The Genius of Busby Berkeley*. Leo Braudy's *The World in a Frame*, published in 1976, the year Berkeley died, brackets the dance director with Eisenstein and Fritz Lang and cites his 'games with continuous narrative' as anticipating the films of the *nouvelle vague*.

Tied to a specific moment, *42nd Street* quickly dated. It was grouped with Warners's 'topical' films in Paul Rotha's and Lewis Jacobs's cinema histories published in the 1930s; and eclipsed in standard accounts of movie musicals by both the Astaire–Rogers films and Arthur Freed's postwar MGM productions. While *42nd Street*'s prominence as a camp artefact suggests a significant subterranean aura, from the mid-60s until the mid-70s the movie's critical reputation was linked to Berkeley's. (As a Lloyd Bacon film, it enjoyed minimal cachet: in *The American Cinema*, Andrew Sarris ranks it number 22, out of 26, on his list of 1933 releases.)

By the time of Berkeley's death, however, *42nd Street* had begun to reassert itself as an essentially authorless work. The movie was seen as a key repository of standard dramatic situations – the 'definitive' (Leonard Maltin, *TV Movies*) or 'archetypal' (Consumers Guide, *The Best, the Worst, & Most Unusual: Hollywood Musicals*) backstage musical, the one that 'gave new life to the clichés that have kept parodists happy' (Pauline Kael, *5000 Nights at the Movies*).

Stanley Donen's 1978 *Movie Movie*, a synthetic double-feature of two mock 30s talkies, including 'Baxter's Beauties of 1933', took the lead in treating *42nd Street* as some sort of classic. While the parody struck Andrew Sarris as stale ('*Dames at Sea* has already done the plot and ethos of Busby Berkeley to a crisp'), Pauline Kael suggested that it was over-reverential. *Movie Movie*, she wrote,

> could use some of that golden hysteria of taking the situation in old movies to a logical extreme, as Charles Ludlam does with the Ridiculous Theatrical Company, putting viewers' secret wild fantasies about the stars and the plot situation right into the story. Clearly the moviemakers wanted to avoid sophistication, satire, and camp.

Thus exorcised of its campiness – and anticipated by several revues based on the music of Harry Warren, including *Mr. Warren's Profession* (London, 1977) and *Lullaby of Broadway* (New York, 1979) – producer David Merrick staged *42nd Street* as a Broadway show, which opened in August 1980. Although the new book simplified the screenplay (while adding a number of songs from subsequent Warners musicals), the $2.5 million production was a suitably Ziegfeldian spectacular, involving 400 costumes and a dozen sets – including electrified backdrops, motorised turntables, a gigantic staircase, and a full-length Pullman car.

This stage *42nd Street*, which appeared in the year that the *42nd*

Street screenplay was published by the University of Wisconsin Press, seemed designed to fulfil the movie's myth. The show had opened on Broadway at last. Like the Warners *42nd Street*, Merrick's appeared during an American Presidential election campaign and a period of relative economic travail. The first run-through was put together for delegates to the Democratic National Convention which renominated President Jimmy Carter. Choreographer Gower Champion died hours before the show opened, necessitating a dramatic announcement by Merrick which followed ten curtain calls and stunned an audience which the *New York Times* characterised as 'extraordinarily glamorous even for an opening night'. To add to the backstage drama, Wanda Richert, who made her Broadway debut as Peggy Sawyer, was keeping company with Champion. 'Life imitated art when Miss Richert herself became an overnight star,' the *Times* reported, hailing Merrick as 'the greatest Broadway showman since Ziegfeld'.

When *42nd Street* closed after 3,486 performances in January 1989, it was the second longest-running musical in Broadway history, behind the not unrelated *A Chorus Line*. (It has since been relegated to third, surpassed by *Cats*.) Among other things, the success of *42nd Street* prompted discussion of a musical based on Busby Berkeley's career; in May 1989, it was reported that the Radio City Music Hall had optioned the rights on John Bernardoni's *Busby*. (The option has yet to be exercised.)

As the celluloid *42nd Street* rationalised the Broadway stage, so the Broadway *42nd Street* (whose run coincided almost exactly with the presidency of Ronald Reagan) reaffirmed the hegemony of the movies, and even Hollywood's imaginary New York. In that, it is a prime example of a vulgar postmodernism – a remake without an original, the revival of a non-existent show.

CREDITS

42nd Street

USA
1933
Production company
Warner Bros Pictures Inc. and the Vitaphone Corporation
US release
23 February 1933
Distributor (US)
Warner Bros–First National
UK release
4 September 1933
Copyright date
29 March 1933

Producer
Darryl F. Zanuck (uncredited)
Production superviser
Hal. B. Wallis (uncredited)
Director
Lloyd Bacon
Dance director
Busby Berkeley
Assistant director
Gordon Hollingshead
Screenplay
Whitney Bolton (uncredited), Rian James, James Seymour from the novel by Bradford Ropes
Photography (black and white)
Sol Polito
Musical direction
Leo F. Forbstein, conducting the Vitaphone Orchestra
Songs
'42nd Street', 'Shuffle off to Buffalo', 'You're Getting to be a Habit with Me', 'Young and Healthy', 'It Must be June' by Al Dubin (lyrics), Harry Warren (music)
Editors
Thomas Pratt, Frank Ware
Art direction
Jack Okey
Costumes
Orry-Kelly (gowns), Cheney Brothers (silks)
89 minutes
8,145 feet

Warner Baxter
Julian Marsh
Bebe Daniels
Dorothy Brock
George Brent
Pat Denning
Ruby Keeler
Peggy Sawyer
Guy Kibbee
Abner Dillon
Una Merkel
Lorraine Fleming
Ginger Rogers
Ann 'Anytime Annie' Lowell
Ned Sparks
Thomas Barry
Dick Powell
Billy Lawler
Allen Jenkins
MacElroy
Edward J. Nugent
Terry Neil
Robert McWade
Al Jones
George E. Stone
Andy Lee
Henry B. Walthall
The actor
Harry Akst
Jerry
Clarence Nordstrom
'Shuffle off to Buffalo' groom
Toby Wing
'Young and Healthy' girl
Al Dubin, Harry Warren
Songwriters
Tom Kennedy
Slim Murphy
Wallis Clark
Dr Chadwick
Jack La Rue
Mug
Louise Beavers
Pansy
Dave O'Brien
Chorus boy
Patricia Ellis
Secretary
George Irving
House doctor

Charles Levison (Charles Lane)
Author
Milton Kibbee
News spreader
Rolfe Sedan
Stage aide
Lyle Talbot
Geoffrey Waring
Harry Seymour
Aide
Kermit Maynard
Dancer
Gertrude Keeler
Helen Keeler
Pat Wing
Geraine Grear (Joan Barclay)
Ann Hovey
Renee Whitney
Dorothy Coonan
Barbara Rogers
June Glory
Jayne Shadduck
Adele Lacy
Loretta Andrews
Margaret La Marr
Mary Jane Halsey
Ruth Eddings
Edna Callaghan
Patsy Farnum
Maxine Cantway
Lynn Browning
Donna Mae Roberts
Lorena Layson
Alice Jans
Eve Marcy
Evelyn Joice
Agnes Ray
Grace Tobin
Chorus girls

The print of *42nd Street* in the National Film Archive was produced from material acquired from Warner Bros. in 1954.

(Credits checked by Markku Salmi)

BIBLIOGRAPHY

Altman, Rick. *The American Film Musical* (Bloomington and London: Indiana University Press and BFI Publishing, 1989)

Altman, Rick (ed.). *Genre: The Musical* (London: Routledge & Kegan Paul/ BFI, 1981). Includes Mark Roth's 'Some Warners Musicals and the Spirit of the New Deal', Lucy Fischer's 'The Image of Woman as Image: The Optical Politics of *Dames*', and Richard Dyer's 'Entertainment and Utopia'

Bergman, Andrew. *We're in the Money: Depression America and Its Films* (New York: Harper and Row, 1972)

Feuer, Jane. *The Hollywood Musical* (London: Macmillan/BFI, 1982)

Fumento, Rocco. 'From Bastards and Bitches to Heroes and Heroines', *42nd Street* (Madison: University of Wisconsin Press, 1980)

Kreuger, Miles (ed.). *The Movie Musical from Vitaphone to 42nd Street* (New York: Dover Publications, 1975)

Mast, Gerald. *Can't Help Singin': The American Musical On Stage and Screen* (Woodstock, NY: Overlook Press, 1987)

Mordden, Ethan. *The Hollywood Musical* (New York: St Martin's Press, 1981)

Pike, Bob, and Martin, Dave. *The Genius of Busby Berkeley* (Reseda Ca: Creative Film Society, 1973)

Roddick, Nick. *A New Deal in Entertainment: Warner Brothers in the 1930s* (London: BFI, 1983)

Schatz, Thomas. *The Genius of the System* (New York: Pantheon Books, 1988)

Thomas, Tony, and Terry, Jim. *The Busby Berkeley Book* (Greenwich, Conn.: New York Graphic Society, 1973)

VANDERBILT
AVE.
E. 42 ST.

BFI Publishing
21 Stephen Street
FREEPOST 7
LONDON
W1E 4AN